STILL

Where would we be without the dedicated
few, both past and present, with enough
curiosity and will to engage with the big
ideas that have made our lives possible?
Sometimes they have braved ridicule or
worse. But their words have taken us on
a collective journey of discovery. This book
is dedicated to those who have dared to
think big and sought to find the beautiful
thread that binds us together.

And to my family, who encourage me
to live *tempo giusto* – the right speed:
sometimes fast, sometimes slow, but always
with a richness of experience that wouldn't
be possible without them.

'Only that day dawns to which we are awake.'

Henry David Thoreau

STILL The Slow Home

Natalie Walton

Photography by Chris Warnes

Hardie Grant

BOOKS

One

CHANGE

15

Two

NOW 97

Three

SLOW 169

STILL

A MOMENT

When were you last still?

Without movement and motion.

And free from thoughts tumbling and rumbling ahead.

But still in the silent depths of quiet calm.

Holding a space for now.

INTRODUCTION

'You are your choices.'   Seneca

We are at the threshold of a defining point in our culture and society. Never before have so many had more than they need. We are consuming at a greater rate than at any other time in history. But with this privilege comes responsibility. And although we can't always control governments or politicians, industry or big business, we can take responsibility for the choices we make within our own lives.

The biggest problems that the world faces are of our own making, and we have the power to create significant change. This can begin today, right now. And there is no easier place to start than at home. There are three important steps to make this possible. The first, and simplest way, is to consume less – it is perhaps the most important tool at our disposal. Secondly, we can also consider the idea of 'localisation', a concept developed by economist Helena Norberg-Hodge, who argues that living locally is one of the most effective countermeasures to globalisation. Our homes are ideally placed to support and promote these ideas, with everything from the materials we source in construction to how we fit out and furnish them. The choices we make don't have to be at the expense of creating a space that feels warm and welcoming, though. Instead, they can actually make us feel better about how and where we live. Thirdly, when we choose to connect more with nature, it becomes a bigger priority in our lives.

But to take these steps we need to become aware of why we have become such voracious consumers. And not just of stuff. Our lives are full to bursting. We spend our days in perpetual motion, chasing lists, deadlines and dreams, and our own expectations.

Hyperconnectivity is making us more stressed and depressed than ever before. In a short period of time we have developed an unhealthy relationship with our devices and their technology, leading us to feel more alone and isolated. All too easily we get caught in reward-seeking loops that can never be satisfied, as we try to get our next hit of dopamine – a potent chemical when it comes to buying goods online. And so our anxiety keeps on growing. As does the quantity of the stuff we have, even though it can never make us feel any better. On the contrary, we often feel worse. Buyer's remorse is one factor, but more powerful is the underlying dissatisfaction that we are not meeting our intrinsic needs.

Our homes are filled with objects we have long since forgotten, and our cupboards crammed with gadgets and homewares that were supposed to save us time or improve our lives. Often we tend to focus on our need for more storage as a solution for containing, and maybe even on some level hiding, our consumerism. However, should we really be asking whether the objects that fill our home are things we actually use or need. It is not uncommon to have rooms that are barely used and, worse still, overflowing with stuff that will get organised 'one day'. Our spaces are often furnished with well-intentioned choices that aren't quite right. It can be the same with our wardrobes. While we may be moving away from fast-fashion chains to more ethical brands – a burgeoning industry of its own – consuming less remains a more sustainable choice because every purchase we make still contributes to the production of 100 billion garments a year, of which about seventy per cent are thrown away. What we buy for our children is part of the problem too; they have more clothes, toys and books, as well as busyness built into their days, than any previous generation.

We have fallen into a trap of focusing on what we perceive is missing from our lives. We spend our days chasing an ideal. Is it any wonder we feel exhausted and overwhelmed, with no energy to consider a different way? Do we really believe that busy is better? That more means more? More opportunities, more money, more happiness? And, conversely, do we think that less means less? Fewer choices, fewer experiences and, perhaps worst of all, that we are less? Less than whom?

The antidote to consumerism is not what we might think, however. What we want is right here. Being present, and aware of how we are living our lives, can help us to make more conscious and informed choices. Living mindfully can also help us to reclaim our life in a way that no consumer good ever can. This moment is the future of what we desired yesterday, last month and last year. And we only ever have this moment to live. The past has already gone and the future is not yet here. However, being present doesn't mean we can't move forward or reach goals. In fact, when we live mindfully we have more clarity and can be more awake to the choices we make. It can also help us to build a pause in the decision-making process. When we reflect upon whether our desire is a want or a need, we can be more intentional with our choices. When we take responsibility for our actions not only do we benefit, but so too does the rest of the world.

Living mindfully is a central tenet of the slow philosophy, which encourages SLOW – Sustainable, Local, Organic, Whole – choices. Yet it is more than thirty years since Carlo Petrini protested against a fast-food chain opening in Rome's Piazza di Spagna, an action that sparked the creation of the slow movement. So, are we eating simpler, working less, sleeping longer, being more community minded?

How can we make positive change in our lives? We can start by asking the right questions – which can help us consider what drives our decisions. When we have a clear understanding of our why, it is much easier to make meaningful change and stay the course. When we simplify from the inside out – rather than attempting quick-fix solutions from the outside in – the changes we embrace become systemic rather than just surface-based. And by communicating about the steps we take, even if we talk to just one person, we can help spread the word and start to change the world.

On the following pages are the stories of twenty couples and individuals from across the globe – over four continents and thirteen countries – who have taken the steps to simplify their lives and embrace the principles of slow living. There is no one way, but many paths that are leading to more awareness and a greater conversation. Some of the stories on these pages are about people who sold off their possessions to reconnect with their lives; others have moved out of the city to embrace a slower pace. There were sea changes and tree changes and cross-continental voyages to be closer to family. Although everyone's journey has been different, home is at the heart of every story.

SIMPLE STEPS TO SLOW LIVING

1 ## Create a vision

Consider how we want to live our lives.
We can only create the life that we can see.

2 ## Develop a value framework

Make meaningful change based on a personal
philosophy – and live by that.

3 ## Find our why

Have a clear sense of purpose to make the
right choices.

4 ## Focus on priorities

Set boundaries around what's most important
in our lives, and allocate our resources
accordingly.

5 ## Take responsibility

Recognise the difference between a need
and a want. And that we have a choice –
from what we consume to how we live.

6 ## Let go

Worry less about how other people are living
their lives. Care less about attaching status
to objects, and measuring them as a sign of
self-worth. Let go to move forward.

7 ## Switch off

Disconnect to reconnect with ourselves
and what matters most. Create community
in real life.

8 ## Live in the now

Become awake to the real beauty of our lives.
Reclaim what's most important.

9 ## Cultivate good feelings

Pay attention to when we feel good or
energised. Cultivate and nurture these
strands of our life.

10 ## Embrace SLOW living one step at a time

Consider Sustainable, Local, Organic,
Whole choices. Develop a rhythm that works
for our lives, and find pleasure in the process.

'Yesterday I was clever, so I wanted to change the world. Today I am wise, so I am changing myself.'

Rumi

CHANGE

Why is it that we change our homes? From moving to renovating, we live in a culture that cannot keep still. And while a lot of good can come from change, we live in a time when it is rare for someone to live in the one home for most of their lives. Houses have become commodities that are bought and sold for quick profit. Decisions are often driven by the bottom line with little regard for their environmental impact. 'Flipping' homes has become part of the vernacular. And television programs have turned the process into a spectator sport, while online entrepreneurs have found ways to monetise quick makeovers that are designed for attention, not the future. Nothing quite catches the collective imagination like a transformation. But at what price?

Many renovations focus on convenience and low cost over quality and longevity. Other times creating a 'look' is given priority with little regard to how quickly it will become outdated. It's an all too common story: in five or ten years' time, materials, fittings and fixtures are replaced not because they have reached the end of their life, but because the look has become tired and the homeowner wants to give the place a makeover. Even when 'dream homes' are sold on, they are not always to everyone's taste – paint schemes are changed, pendant lights replaced and other modifications made to meet a new family's specifications. All of these changes often incur costs that we cannot always count. What becomes of the broken taps, cracked tiles and unwanted carpet? Houses generate more waste than we ever give consideration. When it's out of sight, it's out of mind, although the physical mass hasn't disappeared. Instead, it has been added to a mountain of rubbish – a dump or a landfill site. It's time to take a closer look and become aware of the real cost of our decisions.

We generate around two billion tonnes of waste every year. The globe is covered in landfill sites, some as large as 2200 acres (in Las Vegas, USA) and as high as forty metres (in New Delhi, India). There are also rubbish sites, comprised mainly of plastic, floating in the ocean, such as the Great Pacific Garbage Patch. When it comes to landfill, the focus is not to decompose the waste but to seal it from groundwater and prevent gases from exploding. A new hill might be created in the process, but the rubbish remains. So it is worth asking again. What is the real cost of renovating, and opting for quick and cheap? What is the ultimate price we pay for all of our purchases?

Excess is fast becoming a hallmark of this generation. Today we generate more waste than any other period in history – from food, clothing and electronic waste, to an exorbitant amount of stuff that comes from our homes, and which we should call by its real name: junk. Useless gadgets, gimmicky toys and party miscellany lead a long list. And then there is packaging: almost everything is wrapped in plastic – from produce to pendant lighting, and from notebooks to magazines and newspapers. And be aware that even if you buy goods that aren't packaged in plastic, it's highly likely that it has been present in most of the supply chain. Goods that are sent through online shopping channels – more than 165 billion packages a year in the USA alone – generate significant volumes of plastic and cardboard waste. Globally, the latter equates to more than one billion trees. And the former contributes to the more than 8.3 billion tonnes that have been generated since the 1950s when the mass production of plastics began. The statistics are even more startling when you consider that it takes more than 400 years for plastic to degrade, and that only about nine per cent of all plastic has ever been recycled. We have become disconnected from the impact our decisions make on the world at large.

But what legacy do we want to pass on to our children and future generations? If we are not considering them, then what are we prioritising and why? When it comes to creating and updating our homes, we should consider the actual cost of change. And our underlying motivations. What is it we are really seeking?

CREATE A VISION

We can live more responsibly within our homes when we consider that our decisions have an impact not just on the world today but on the form it will take tomorrow. If we have a choice, we also have power. This position of privilege is something we should acknowledge and respect. It can inform the vision of the world we want to create and the journey that's needed to make it possible. So let's consider our legacy. What mark do we want to leave on the world? How do we want to be remembered? What gift do we have to give? To this end, we can consider the Japanese concept of *ikigai* – a reason for being. It is based upon the idea of what we consider to be of value in our lives and what gives them meaning. Interestingly, the word *ikigai* has its origins in the Japanese island of Okinawa, which is said to have the largest population of centenarians in the world. In many ways they embody the principles of slow living: they stay active but in a gentle way, eat well but are not gluttonous, connect to those around them but also spend time alone in nature, and live in the moment. Let us consider the contribution that we want to make. What do we want our legacy to be? When it comes to our homes, can we create them in a way that makes a positive contribution – buildings and spaces that others want to maintain or preserve, for example? Can we embrace choices that will withstand trends or at least won't deplete the world's resources irreparably? Our vision is our guide and compass to living in a way that is more aligned with our values.

DEVELOP A VALUE FRAMEWORK

When we gravitate towards making change in our lives, we do so in the hope that they will be better. But how do we know which path to take? We all want to make the right decisions. We find our way when we establish the same framework for our lives as for the homes we're creating. First, we envisage the big picture, then lay the foundations and build the framework to make improvements step by step. When it comes to our lives, once we have created a vision, we should consider what we stand for – our personal value system – and this becomes the framework that guides our decision-making.

So what do we value? What is most important? For many of us, it might be family or the future, but it can also be nature or community. We can value more than one element, although sometimes we have to prioritise one over another. But we can feel empowered about making positive change by cross-checking against our list of values when making decisions on everything from where we live, the size of our home, the materials we use, and the items we choose to furnish it with. When narrowing down our choices, we can check to see if we are honouring the elements of our lives that we say are important. For example, when it comes to choosing flooring, we can prioritise a more sustainable choice by using recycled floorboards or ones certified by the Forest Stewardship Council (FSC). We can also choose to live plastic- or waste-free. When we create using our values as a guide, our homes can become more meaningful.

FIND OUR WHY

Even when we have a clear understanding of what we value, it is easy to become overwhelmed with the options on offer. We are deluged with ideas and information. We can become distracted too by the flood of details about other people's lives. Little wonder we can experience decision fatigue on everything from where to live, how much to spend on a home, whether to extend or work within a building's footprint, to the materials to choose for a kitchen benchtop, finishes for a floor and the handles for a door. If we take a moment to understand the motivations behind our decisions, we are more likely to make the right ones. We can do this easily when we ask 'why' in relation to any question. It is a way to discover our intention or true sense of purpose – and we are more likely to make the right decisions.

Having a clear understanding of our why on any decision we make also allows us to start trusting our gut instincts. Research shows that these are actually better decisions too. What is right for someone else is not necessarily right for our situation. So while it can be easy to know *what* we want to do and *how*, as well as *when* we want to do it, we should also understand *why* we want to go down a particular path.

'Why' is a question that should be asked in relation to some of the biggest and smallest decisions of our daily lives, and before we make any purchase. *Why am I really doing this?* If we say we want to care more for the environment, let's dig deeper before we make a purchase, even a 'sustainable' one. We may just discover an unexpected intention. And to get a deeper understanding of our intention, we can ask 'why' five times. Often we are trying to meet a desire, not a need. When we have a clear sense of our why, decision-making is easier, as is staying the course.

FOCUS ON PRIORITIES

Once we have a clear understanding of our values and purpose, we can set boundaries around how we live our lives. There is often a great disparity between the life we want to live and how we spend our days. Our attention and self-control are under siege from the moment we wake until just before sleep. Ask anyone what matters most to them and the answer is easy. However, if we look at how we spend our time, our days are filled with contradictions. The data is clear. We are addicted to our devices. We know the truth even if we sometimes struggle to admit it. Yet how much time do we spend completely engaged with our family on a daily basis? And are we really prioritising the planet when we make purchases on a regular basis, even 'sustainable' or 'ethical' ones?

Our homes are ideally placed to create boundaries. Devices can be left at the front door, and mealtimes and gatherings reserved for real-life connection. Bedrooms can also be preserved as sanctuaries from technology. Let's care more about what we value and care less about what's not worth our time or money. And give careful thought to when to say yes and when to say no. The more we set boundaries around what matters most in our lives and live intentionally, the more we can live in alignment with our priorities.

TAKE RESPONSIBILITY

Let's consider who benefits most from many of our daily decisions. Global corporations with billion-dollar profits know the answer. It's good to question if what we desire is a need or a want before we make any purchase. We can also build a pause into our decision-making process. Do we need to move house or build a bigger one? Do we need to make structural or cosmetic changes? And if we do, can we make them more responsibly? Is there a more sustainable choice? Can we wait? Are we opting for timeless choices that will withstand trends? Throughout the world, previous generations built structures and furniture, rugs, pots and much more in a slow and considered way. These buildings and objects have lasted hundreds and sometimes thousands of years. Given all we have access to, is this not still possible?

We also have the ability to choose our response – from what we believe to how we behave. We can cultivate self-awareness. Pay attention, be proactive and do the work. Small steps lead to consistent results. Good habits yield good results. We should take responsibility for the energy we bring to a space or situation, too.

TEN WAYS TO MAKE POSITIVE CHANGE FOR THE PLANET

1   Consume less. Or borrow if we need something only once or occasionally. Repair or repurpose what we already own. And make sure we buy goods that come with warranties and have parts that can be replaced.

2   Buy second-hand. Consider vintage wares, estate sales, antique shops, salvage yards, flea markets, car boot sales, online marketplaces, charity shops, yard sales or roadside finds, which technically cost us nothing.

3   Shop local and support local businesses. Save on food miles and carbon footprints. Plus, by supporting local business, you are fostering community.

4   Reduce waste. Purchase goods with less packaging, and ask shop owners about their supply chain. Buy in bulk, and take containers. Re-use spray bottles, glass jars and other reusables. Use a cloth instead of paper towel, napkins instead of paper serviettes, metal straws instead of paper or plastic. Recycle, including soft plastic. Compost food scraps or feed to the chickens.

5   Eat more veggies. Eating less meat and dairy is the biggest and simplest ways to reduce our environmental impact on the planet.

6   Be energy efficient. Turn off and unplug lights, electronic devices and appliances when not in use to save on power. Also, turn on power-save mode on computers and other electronic equipment. Use energy-efficient appliances and light bulbs. Opt for cold water cycles on washing machines to reduce energy consumption, and line dry clothes.

7   Use renewable energy. Install solar panels if possible. But also find out if your energy provider uses renewable energy sources. Also, check if your pension or superannuation fund makes ethical and sustainable investments.

8   Be water smart. Install a more efficient shower head and dual-flush toilet. Take shorter showers and flush less. Capture rainwater in a tank. Only wash clothes when necessary and divert grey water to the garden. Place bowls in the kitchen sink and under leaking taps to catch water for veggie beds.

9   Plant trees. Grow a native, succulent or drought-tolerant garden.

10   Embrace slow travel. Reduce your carbon emissions on journeys to and from home – walk, cycle, carpool, take public transport or use electric or hybrid vehicles.

Simple steps can make significant change.

NINA & CRAIG PLUMMER

Edinburgh, Scotland

'This home is our little escape from the world. It's where we can be ourselves. It's where we can relax.'

At the start of every year, Nina and Craig Plummer reflect on the one that has passed and consider areas for improvement. In January 2016, while living in London, they came to realise that some areas of their life were out of balance. 'London is an amazing bustling place,' Nina says. 'However, we were both working long hours, travelling a lot as part of our daytime jobs, and we had just started a business and didn't have enough time for each other, our friends and family or to enjoy life. Everything in London happens at quite a quick pace and we wanted a slightly slower way of living.'

The realisation became a catalyst for the decision to move back to Scotland, where they had met while at university. They hoped to buy and renovate a home there, plus the move would allow them to be closer to Craig's family. With a population of only 500,000 compared with London's eight million, Edinburgh is a significantly smaller city, yet it is the second largest financial centre in the United Kingdom. This was appealing for Craig, who works in finance. And for Nina, a former psychologist, the plan would allow her to focus on the couple's homewares business, Ingredients LDN.

The move to Edinburgh has been a good one, offering them a better quality of life in many ways. Instead of spending hours commuting, Craig walks to work and feels he has a better work–life balance. And even though their flat is in the heart of the city, they are still close to nature. At the end of the street they have shared keyholder access to a seven-acre private gated garden. And one of their favourite beaches, Tyninghame, is only about forty minutes away. 'We both enjoy spending time outdoors and being connected to nature; in London we had to travel quite far to do that,' Nina says. Plus, they enjoy living within the wide and generous 200-year-old New Town streets, which are considered a masterpiece of city planning and have been listed as part of a UNESCO World Heritage site.

When they first relocated from London to Scotland, they moved into Craig's parents' place in Fife while they looked for somewhere to buy. After searching for almost six months, they found a first-floor drawing room flat in an 1816 Georgian sandstone townhouse. They bought it in June 2017, but the wait still wasn't over. Because it's a Grade A listed building – the most protected type – they had to apply for permissions to make internal changes. One of the benefits, though, was that they were able to get funding towards restoring the windows. It took about seven months to gain permission to commence renovations, and most of the work was completed within three months.

The appeal of the place was worth the wait and the hard work. 'We wanted to be central in New Town and it had to be a Georgian property,' Nina says. 'There are some beautiful Victorian buildings in the West End but I love Georgian architecture. I also wanted this exact style of window. They are big with six by nine astragals and let in lots of light. And the rooms had beautiful four-metre-high ceilings.'

'These type of properties are not easy to come by,' Craig says. 'They are very much in demand.' The couple also wanted a place that was unrenovated, and this place delivered. 'The flat was a mess,' Craig says. 'The lady who lived here was a hoarder and she'd been here for about fifteen years.' The living room ceiling was painted apricot, and the windows were framed with tartan curtains and pelmets. Floral wallpaper covered the walls in the bathroom, which was located in the site of the current kitchen. The entrance hallway was salmon pink and the bedroom cornflower blue. Many of the walls and ceilings featured woodchip wallpaper, which took the couple many weekends to strip back.

However, before they even found the flat they knew the style of kitchen they wanted – one made of sustainable beechwood by deVOL. Custom modifications were made at the couple's request, such as castor wheels to enable a moveable island bench. The kitchen area was also enlarged and the bathroom relocated into a smaller third bedroom.

Overall, Nina and Craig wanted a calm, neutral space. They prioritised natural materials such as wood, marble, ceramic, linen and wool. 'We spent a lot of time thinking about how to create a space that would still look good in ten years' time,' Nina says. And while it was important to create a space where they could relax, they also wanted the flexibility to be able to socialise and entertain. 'We wanted it to suit our lifestyle and to make it more comfortable,' Nina says.

When I do less…
I feel at ease. If I'm rushed, I feel more stressed.

When I disconnect…
I feel more at peace, more in the moment.

I have learnt to live without…
a television. We have been living without one
for about seven years. We got rid of it when we
moved to London. And even though we're of
the generation that has grown up with social
media, we don't use it for our personal lives,
only for our business.

I set boundaries around…
time. That's something we're increasingly doing.
We've come to realise that we have to allocate
time mindfully for the things that matter most.
Otherwise, it's too easy to do a little bit of
everything but ultimately not much of anything
of true value.

Calm is…
the weekend. Being together on the weekend.

Change is…
exciting. It's been a constant in our lives
because we've moved around quite a lot.

When it comes to order and chaos
in our life…
we try to find a balance between both. It feels
as if there are periods when we embrace or even
seek out the chaos and then there are times
when we feel the pull to slow things down
before ultimately embracing the next challenge.
This is how we experience the ebb and flow of
chaos and order in our life.

I care less about…
what is expected of me. The older we get the
more we feel confident to carve out our own way.
There are a lot of things that are expected in life
and we have come to realise that we don't have to
do any of them, which is quite empowering.

I care more about…
the people in my life. When we consider what is
most meaningful to us as people, and therefore
what drives us as a species, it's not the things we
own but the connections we have with others.

My life feels meaningful when…
I'm with Craig. Increasingly, we are setting
goals for our life. We're moving more towards
a particular lifestyle. There's something really
nice when we catch a glimpse of a particular
area of life that we've worked very hard on and
see that we have achieved it together.

What's most important in our life
right now is…
working towards balance. We often find that life
is a continuous process of falling out of balance
and then finding our way back to it. So much of
what we are working towards at the moment is
about mastering that rhythm.

**EMBRACING SLOW –
SUSTAINABLE, LOCAL, ORGANIC, WHOLE:**

Sustainable living means…
thoughtful living, which is definitely an
iterative process. There's nothing fixed about
what it means because the world is changing
so quickly. If it's too prescriptive, it can be
problematic. It's similar to the life philosophy
of letting our values guide everything we do
and yet not allowing ourselves to become too
rigid in our thinking – to me this flexibility and
willingness to change feels very sustainable.

Local is…
about human connection. So much of my work
life is based online. Being part of this global
community has many benefits. However, it's
important to feel a sense of connection to the
people in our local community too.

Organic is…
what we really love. We prefer when objects
aren't perfect, when they're not even, and
when they're not mass-produced. When every
form isn't identical it has a little more soul.
We have the same association with food –
not everything has to be perfect and uniform.

I feel Whole when…
I'm with the people I love.

FINDING OUR TRUTH

How can we navigate our way through this time of mass consumerism, information and image overload? And how can shop owners become part of the solution? Nina Plummer, of Ingredients LDN, studied psychology at Dundee University, Scotland, after growing up in Vienna, Austria. Here she reflects on how we can take a more thoughtful approach to homemaking.

Nina Plummer

We find ourselves at a time and place in this world, at once challenging and rich in potential. Our attention, brazenly commoditised and increasingly divided, is flooded with so much information and so many choices that we are often left feeling overwhelmed and exhausted rather than empowered.

We are required to process more options and decide between more possibilities than ever before. And while this status quo places us in what is arguably the most privileged position in history, to make use of this privilege requires that we develop the skills necessary for identifying those choices that are right for us.

With so many options on offer and a plethora of media channels presenting daily snippets of the polished lives of others, it can be easy to succumb to the ever-growing pressure to keep up. Without a clear sense of what we want and why, it can often feel safest to follow where everyone else is going. But not all paths that have been glamorised by current cultural trends are necessarily the right path for us.

Following others, detached from a defined sense of self, can leave us feeling hollow and vulnerable, convinced that happiness is just around the corner, hidden from view by the next achievement, acquisition or change in circumstance. In this challenging environment, learning how to make our own decisions with confidence and self-assuredness is an invaluable skill.

Upon deep and honest reflection, how many of us can answer with any precision what we truly want out of life and why? Even more so, how many of us can say how the answer to this question translates into what we do and the decisions we make on a daily basis?

In a frantic world with too many strains on our attention, slower living is about choosing to engage with life more mindfully. It is about allowing ourselves the time to become aware of what is most important in life and why. It is about cultivating an understanding of what we value most and about using these values to guide how our day-to-day lives unfold.

Becoming intimately familiar with the fabric of our own being is a life's work. Like any practice, it requires time, dedication and endurance. At the heart of this endeavour lies the ability to sit still, undistracted, for long enough to discover what moves us most. The 'slow' in slow living is not necessarily about temporality. Instead, much of this approach to life rests on taking the time to become aware, to process what is happening in our lives and to understand how we feel and why. A dedication to this practice is what allows us to build a strong sense of self, becoming ever clearer about what is right for us and why.

The better we become at understanding what we want out of life and why, the less tempting the myriad other choices become and the more likely we are

Nina Plummer

to recognise and appreciate the small steps taken on the path towards building a life that is right for us. Gratitude is the best inoculation against discontent. And in a world that can often feel highly incentivised to cultivate our perpetual dissatisfaction, this inoculation is a welcome remedy.

The benefits of becoming intimately familiar with our own sense of self are subtle at first but ever greater the more we invest in this practice. And if we allow ourselves the time, cultivating a reflective practice can begin to serve as the bedrock for almost all decision-making. Ultimately, the fruits of this labour can guide our goals and dreams for the future, what we learn and how we spend our free time, what we say yes to and what we say no to and, most importantly, how we conduct ourselves in relationship to ourselves and others.

An intimate understanding of how we want to live and how this translates into the decisions we make on a daily basis can even be used as a guide for how we create our homes.

The flood of options available today has not left the domain of home decor untouched. Swept up in the tempestuous current of fast fashion, interior trends seem to come and go at an ever-increasing pace. But a growing number of people, swimming against this current, are opting for a more thoughtful approach to homemaking.

We can create homes driven by the desire to achieve a specific 'look'. But this approach leaves us vulnerable to the whims of changing fashion trends. Rather than simply focusing on how our spaces ought to look, an alternative approach is to allow the design of our homes to be guided by an understanding of the life we want to unfold within them.

Trends come and go and what looks good today most likely won't look as good in ten years' time. But if we design our homes to facilitate how we want to live and how we want to feel within them, we are far more likely to stay content through changing trends. Rather than only looking outwards for ideas and inspiration, this attitude towards design is informed by a more reflective approach: one based on an understanding of what we value and how we want to live and feel, independent of what everyone else is doing.

An indiscriminate pursuit of trends and an attitude of disposability have had a significant impact, not only on our planet but on our own sense of wellbeing. As a consequence, a more conscious approach to consumption is now starting to emerge. Increasingly guided by values rather than trends and a clear understanding of what will serve them well and bring them joy for longer, people are adopting a more intentional approach to what they buy.

Consumption of previous decades has relied on stoking our inherent tendency to become dissatisfied with what we have, fostering the urge to keep up with others. Consumption of the future will rely more heavily on providing people with the knowledge and information they need to make choices they will be satisfied with for longer.

As a shopkeeper, I feel it is both a privilege and a responsibility to be able to make a contribution towards this shift. An important part of the service I can provide is to take the time to discover and tell the stories behind the objects we offer. I want to promote quality and longevity over seasonal changes and to highlight the inherent value in material and craft, and in the people behind the products in our shop. I want to participate in fostering a more mindful approach to consumption and in cultivating an aesthetic that emphasises the beauty in imperfection and individual differences over homogeneity.

Slower living is about allowing ourselves the time to engage more mindfully with all aspects of daily life. The choices we make with regard to what objects we buy and how we design our homes may be less important when compared to the vast array of truly meaningful life decisions we have to make. But an intimate understanding of the self and what we value most in life can work in service of both. It can serve as a guide for decisions on how we run our businesses, how we raise our families and, yes, even life's luxuries, like how we design our homes.

When we make decisions mindfully, informed by our values and based on an intimate familiarity with the self, our decisions are more likely to lead us to a life richer in pleasure, fulfilment and meaning. Whether these decisions are big or small, vital or a luxury, our choices and actions begin to come together to weave the fabric of a life well lived.

NINA PLUMMER spent several years working as a clinical psychologist, helping people who were experiencing depression and anxiety. She has also spent time consulting to brands on strategy and consumer insights. Ingredients LDN, which she founded in 2016 in London, brings some of the key lessons from both industries. She has created a concept store that not only promotes wares that can enhance our experiences every day, but also shares ideas and starts conversations about the journey to wellbeing.

JOÃO RODRIGUES

Lisbon, Portugal

'Home is our sacred space. It's a place that we share with our loved ones. And it's where we can relax and enjoy our lives. Nothing is imposed upon us in this space – and that's one of its beauties.'

About twelve years ago, João Rodrigues embarked on a journey of transforming family homes into places to share with visitors from all over the world. The first project was Casas na Areia, a beach house in Comporta on the coast of Portugal that was converted into cabins in collaboration with architect Manuel Aires Mateus. 'This made me understand that if you do it right, you end up building not just a house but a small destination where people want to stay,' João says. He also noticed that the architecture of the space can affect how people respond to their surroundings. In Casas na Areia, the floor of the main living and dining areas are made of sand. 'We understood that we wanted more than a house – we wanted to create places where people could relax, reconnect and spend time with their loved ones,' he says. 'We wanted to create unique spaces and moments where people could have time for themselves, where they wouldn't be distracted and could focus on themselves and those they love.'

Santa Clara 1728 is João's fourth project with Manuel under the umbrella Silent Living. It is also his home and where he lives with his wife Andreia and their five children, João, fifteen, Maria, thirteen, Helena, eight, António, six, and baby Augusto. João, an international airline pilot, purchased the eighteenth-century building about five years ago. The original plan was to renovate and turn it into boutique accommodation after guests at his other properties asked for recommendations on where to stay in Lisbon, Portugal's historic capital city. Located on the doorstep of Alfama, a cultural and historic quarter within the city, the house overlooks the Tagus River and the seventeenth-century church and monastery São Vicente de Fora. It is in one of the few areas that wasn't affected by a devastating earthquake that struck the city in 1755, destroying large parts of Lisbon and the surrounding towns.

Not long after restoration work began on the building, João's daughter Helena made a comment that changed the course of the project, and his

family life. He had taken her to see the construction site. 'I like to do this so they value the people who are doing the work, and for them to see how long it takes,' João says. 'She was about five years old and said, "Dad, this house is so beautiful. When are we moving in?"' That night he told his wife the story and Andreia said she also loved it. At the time, the family were living in another part of Lisbon, about a twenty-minute drive to the city centre. 'But you never said anything,' he responded. 'I want to live there too.'

The couple sat down with their architect and re-evaluated the project. They decided to live on the top floor and convert the roof attic into bedrooms for the children. The plan was quite simple, and in keeping with the look and feel of the other projects João had completed with Manuel. They were all based on the idea that the buildings would be as close to the original structure as possible. The facade of Santa Clara was maintained and supported with a metal frame, while the interior was rebuilt. During the restoration, the builders found the numbers 1728 engraved over the main door. João believes this is the original date of the building, but can't be certain because most of the house's documents were lost during the earthquake. However, it is a detail that pays homage to the past. Honouring the memory of Portuguese architectural history is an important element in each project.

Embracing simplicity is another hallmark of the homes. Originally the plan for Santa Clara was to create fifteen guest rooms, but this number was reduced to ten, and then to six because João wanted all of them to face the river. He and Manuel distilled the spaces again, and Santa Clara now has six guest rooms on the first floor, with his family home on the top two floors. 'We wanted to honour the idea that space is comfort and provides a level of freedom to enjoy privacy,' he says.

Prioritising local materials has played an important role in each project, and is a way to create connections to a sense of place. 'There is incredible craftsmanship in Portugal,' João says. As much as possible, he tries to source all of the materials from within a half-hour radius of the site. This is true of the pine floorboards, limestone from Pêro Pinheiro, near Sintra, and ceramic tiles in the bathrooms. Each element also acts as a sensory stimulant, adding to the atmosphere of the home. The limestone baths, for example, feel both ancient and modern. They start off as huge blocks that are carved and hand-polished over two to three days. 'The idea was that the building shouldn't have anything within it that wouldn't be able to last another 300 years,' João says.

There are many other ways in which each home is connected to the local area. The eighteenth-century painting that features in the Santa Clara dining room was found in an antique shop on the opposite side of the street. Originally the room was going to have floor-to-ceiling shelving, but when João saw the artwork, he changed the plans, to have only two shelves, allowing the painting to take centre stage.

Elevating the role of family is another key ingredient. Sitting together at mealtimes is an important ritual in João's home. In Continental Europe, where breakfast is often just a quick coffee, they spend at least half an hour eating together. When not flying, João enjoys spending time with guests downstairs, too. 'I find it very enriching to meet other people,' he says. 'That is also one of my fuels.' And he feels that the people who visit add to the spirit of the home as well.

Within his own apartment, João embraces simplicity, even with five young children. 'I believe children do what we do,' he says. 'They don't do what we tell them. I am always tidy and like things organised, and they tend to do that too.' Because he travels a lot for work, he prefers interiors that feel calm. 'When I get home, I want to feel that I can slow down,' he says. Ultimately, João believes that when we have less, we can live more.

João Rodrigues

When I do less…
I feel I am missing out. On meeting me, people say I'm a calm person, but my mind never stops.

When I disconnect…
I feel alive. I do it often.

I have learnt to live without…
crowds. I love being with people one to one, but don't enjoy being with too many people.

I set boundaries around…
the amount of work I do. That's one of the things I always have to limit with myself. It's one of the excesses I feel sometimes.

Calm is…
something that helps me focus. When I calm down that's the time when I'm most focused.

Change is…
beautiful. I love change. I am one of those people who always want to make improvements. And while I'm not the best person to ensure that everything gets done, I enjoy thinking of ways we can do things better and having workshops with the team every month to make them happen.

When it comes to order and chaos in my life…
I tend to strive for order, but sometimes I end up in the middle of chaos.

I care less about…
what other people think and what other people do. That can be quite tricky nowadays; you want to keep the line of your projects and not get distracted by what other people are doing.

I care more about…
family and the people who are close to me. I am one of those people who has to help. Generally, I have a people-orientated and not a goal-orientated mind.

My life feels meaningful when…
I am making other people happy. That's the aim of my life. I'm happy whenever people around me are happy.

What's most important in my life right now is…
my family, and not only the people who live in my house but also my parents, siblings and the family who I work with and the people who come to stay with us. I also love having new projects in my life, rethinking the process again.

**EMBRACING SLOW –
SUSTAINABLE, LOCAL, ORGANIC, WHOLE:**

Sustainable living means…
using local materials when rebuilding. Not only does it honour the architecture and the past that has been part of this 300-year-old building, but it also makes the whole story right because you don't transform a place like this, you give it a different usage.

Local is…
the customs we have – they can relate to food or even how we welcome people. I always like to tell this story: when someone comes to your house for the first time they probably have access to the living room and dining room. But in Portugal, if someone visits your house for the first time, we show them everything – the bedroom, the bathroom, the kitchen – it's the local way. What we aim for when we do it is to make other people feel at home.

Organic is…
related to the idea of connection. Most of the furniture has been handmade, such as the table downstairs. It is six metres long and was made by a carpenter who brought it in his van. Then it was mounted and finished with beeswax. It's this idea of connection with craft.

I feel Whole when…
I have moments of incredible happiness. A few months ago I took one of my children on a trip, and as we were coming back home and I was putting the key in the door, he said, 'I want to tell you one thing before you open the door. The most beautiful thing that I have in my life are the times when there is just the two of us.' That was one of those beautiful moments.

KINE ASK STENERSEN & KRISTOFFER ENG

Drammen, Norway

'We just want an everyday life that we're happy in – a balanced life. The vibe is slower here in this neighbourhood. Starting our business has also been a decision on how can we slow down. How can we do something we love but also be with our family, and be more in charge of our time.'

Changing the pace of life and priorities were big but important steps towards starting a family and a business for Kine Ask Stenersen and Kristoffer Eng. About five years ago, the couple packed up their apartment in Oslo, Norway, and moved back to the area in which they had both grown up. Drammen, an industrial port city only forty minutes from the capital, is becoming increasingly popular as a place to live for young families who want to enjoy more space and fewer financial obligations. For Kine and Kristoffer it was also an opportunity to be closer to their parents, who enjoy helping to look after the couple's two young sons, Vilmer, four, and Artur, one. The move has enabled them to launch their own business, Ask og Eng, which specialises in custom-made sustainable kitchens and furniture.

Kine and Kristoffer were looking to buy a place with character, high ceilings and lots of light. What they found was a 1932 two-storey timber house with a garden and district views. 'There aren't too many of these types of houses,' Kine says. 'We didn't want something that had been recently renovated because this is where we are going to stay, so we wanted a place we could make our own.'

Since moving into the house they have opened up many of the rooms, widened doorways and added a bathroom and bedroom. But it has been a slow process. 'We have mostly renovated it bit by bit, but we've also done a few larger areas all at once,' Kine says. They moved in during the summer of 2014 and the plan was to have the place liveable by October. However, Vilmer was born two months early when they still didn't have electricity or hot water in the house. As it was getting colder, they moved to a family cabin for a few weeks while key jobs were completed. It was a tough time for them. The cabin was basic and they had to cart water from a well. 'We had a newborn baby and I was struggling with breastfeeding,' Kine says. 'I remember sitting in front of the fire and trying to keep warm.'

When the couple returned to the house, essential services were in place but the renovation was still far from finished. 'Instead of relaxing while the baby was sleeping, I prioritised painting even though I was so tired,' Kine says. 'I needed to get it done so we could be in a calm home and a clean, tidy space. I couldn't relax in such a chaotic environment.'

Since then they have slowly worked on different areas of the home. 'It's been a continual process,' Kine says. 'And there hasn't been a clear plan. I prefer to follow my gut feelings,' she says. 'I'm guided more by a general sense of what I want our home to be – to create a place where we can relax, where I enjoy being, particularly as I work from home.'

It was while Kristoffer, an architect, and Kine, an environmental geographer, were working on the renovations that an idea formed to create a business together. They launched Ask og Eng in 2016 after building sustainable bamboo kitchens both in their Oslo apartment and later in the Drammen house. Initially they made everything at their home, but the business outgrew the space and is now based in a local workshop that's within walking distance.

Creating their own products has given them a new appreciation for the true value of handmade objects. 'When we renovated this place, we wanted to find sustainable solutions but found that it was really hard to source suitable materials,' Kine says. 'We wondered why these things weren't more accessible, so we had to do lots of research. That then became a key part of our business – to make sustainable options more accessible to everyone.'

'Good materials always get better over time, too,' Kristoffer says. 'Plus, you tend to care more for objects that you value.' The couple's home has been created based on these principles. To furnish their home, they took a trip to Denmark to visit second-hand stores. That's how they found the pendant that hangs above their dining table. They still remember the drive and having lunch in a park before finding it. 'Hopefully our kids will have it too, because it's a classic and also has a great story to it,' Kine says. 'It's valuable in another way.' Similarly, they try to make sustainable choices with other areas of their home. 'Now we know how much work goes into making something by hand, we appreciate these things more,' Kine says. 'We appreciate it in our own way.'

When I do less…
I feel good. When I take time out and have
a break from everything, I have more energy.

When I disconnect…
I feel better. My work is so involved with
technology and sitting in front of a screen
that I began to realise I needed to disconnect;
otherwise, it's too hard to unwind properly.

I have learnt to live without…
a sense of obligation. Now I only accept
invitations that are meaningful for me.
Since running a business and having young
children, I need to be more considered
about how I prioritise my time.

I set boundaries around…
different areas of my life. Before I had all kinds
of illusions. Now I live more in accordance
with what I want to do, prioritising time to
spend it with people who give me energy and
genuinely like and love me.

Calm is…
something I experience when I'm travelling.
I've travelled a lot in my life. However, I don't
need to go far to experience that sense of
calmness. Kristoffer says there's a Kine and
a 'Cabin Kine' – the person I become when
I visit a summer cabin. I need to get away
because that's when I discover my calm self.

Change is…
great. I don't like a routined life. I'm always
evolving. I'm always seeking change.

When it comes to order and chaos
in my life…
at times it can feel very chaotic, because I have
a lot of things going on in my life. But I am
quite organised. While I need our home to be
tidy, Kristoffer needs it to be clean. Because
it's so chaotic in my head, I need our home to
be organised. The house might look tidy, but
when you look inside the cupboards it's a bit
of a mess.

I care less about…
what people think. Over the last couple of
years I have met many great and inspiring
people who are all doing their own thing,
and to me that's been very liberating.
There are so many ways to live.

I care more about…
finding balance between doing what I love
and family life.

My life feels meaningful when…
I am with my family and when I get to
be creative.

What's most important in my life
right now is…
my family.

**EMBRACING SLOW –
SUSTAINABLE, LOCAL, ORGANIC, WHOLE:**

Sustainable living means…
embracing the whole version of it. We try to
care about the environment in many small
and practical ways. Let's all do what we can.
And vote for politicians who can make positive
change possible.

Local is…
a big part of our everyday life. We have our
production workshop and studio here.

Organic is…
important in different ways. Organic is how
it was originally. Its natural state of being. We
try to work in this way – not adding artificial
extras, but keeping it real and clean – whether
it's the materials we use, the food we eat, the
clothes we wear or the soaps we use.

I feel Whole when…
I experience enough calm but also get enough
change and activity.

ALEJANDRO STICOTTI
& MERCEDES HERNÁEZ

Buenos Aires, Argentina

'Every day I say "thank you" for being able to
live here. It is like living in a garden.'

When Alejandro Sticotti and Mercedes Hernáez
were searching for a home in the leafy Buenos Aires
suburb of Olivos more than a decade ago, they
didn't expect to buy a garden. Initially they had gone
to view an English-style house in the area, but it was
too dark inside. The real estate agent suggested they
offer to buy the neighbouring garden, a plot of land
shared by the two houses. 'Getting a piece of land
in this area is almost impossible,' Alejandro says.
'We loved the idea. A 15-metre by 35-metre lot in
Olivos – incredible!' The couple bought the land
with a view that Alejandro, an architect, would
design the home.

'It was our first house together so it has a lot of
significance,' Mercedes says. 'We wanted to create a
new life together.' While Mercedes found the design
and build process long, she has no complaints about
the finished result. 'It is magic to live here,' she says.

It took three years to complete the build – from
the project phase to construction and finalising all
the details. 'Everything is tailor-made,' Alejandro
says. 'I basically lived on the construction site back
then.' He designed the home around simple 'noble
materials' – metal, concrete and wood – without any
paint or coatings. 'However, it's hard to make your
own house,' he says. 'The temptation is to include
everything you like, and you want everything to be
perfect. And you're always thinking I should have
done that better. But I love the house; it's getting
better with age.'

Since its completion eight years ago, the exterior
timber has started to silver off and the trees have
grown to embrace the house. 'That's what's nice
about this place,' Alejandro says. 'It's like living in the
woods because you can see greenery everywhere.'

The couple live a thirty-minute drive from their
joint space of the Sticotti design studio and Mono
shop in Palermo, an inner-city neighbourhood of
Buenos Aires. Mercedes, a graphic designer, also
works from her home-based timber-lined studio.
Across the corridor from the studio are a series of
rooms where their four grown children, Joaquin,
twenty-nine, Lucca, twenty-five, Milo, twenty-three
and Violet, twenty-one, stay when visiting. The
couple also have two dogs who seem to enjoy the
house as much as they do, and can often be found
basking in the sun and sleeping on the sofa.

'The house has a strong structure – which
represents Alejandro – but the mood mostly
represents me,' Mercedes says. It is most evident in
the living room and garden, she explains. 'And the
studio is my place.'

'We love art and design,' Alejandro says. 'Our lives
are dedicated to them. Everything in this house was
chosen with aesthetic and functional criteria in mind.'

Mercedes collects textiles, and often takes special
blankets from their home in Olivos to their holiday
house in Uruguay. 'They are not ordinary blankets –
they might have been made in Peru or have some
other special memory attached to them – so it's
important that I have them close by,' she says. She
feels the same way about certain books, notebooks
and pencils. 'They show who I was when I was
drawing or writing in that year. I realise who I am
when I draw – I feel a little bit more alive,' she says.

The kitchen is the vibrant functioning heart
of the house, because that's where they spend
most of their time. 'I love to cook – more than my
wife,' Alejandro says. He designed the space into
separate zones: a preparation area and another area
dedicated to cooking. 'It's small but it's complete,'
he says. 'I like that it's integrated with the house;
it's not another room. And it has a nice view.'

However, the living room is Mercedes' sanctuary.
She enjoys relaxing on the sofa and looking out
to the garden. 'That's where I have breakfast, read,
draw and embroider,' she says. 'That's my nest.'

They both enjoy working in the garden, a space
where they often spend time together, especially
on weekends. What set their journey in motion to
live in Olivos is now an integral part of their lived
experience. 'It's nice to live in nature,' Mercedes says.
Even – or perhaps, especially – when their patch is
only a short drive from the city. Mercedes says she
could never live amongst the bustle again, preferring
a more tranquil existence. 'Here you are in touch
with nature and the cycle of the seasons.'

Alejandro Sticotti & Mercedes Hernáez

... and then I asked
him with my eyes to
ask again yes
and then he asked
me would I yes...
and first I put my
arms around him yes
and drew him down
to me so he could
feel my breasts all
perfume yes
and his heart was
going like mad
and yes I said yes
I will Yes.

Alejandro Sticotti & Mercedes Hernáez

    Alejandro Sticotti & Mercedes Hernáez

When I do less…

I feel more inspired. I choose my clients
well and I prefer to work only on projects
I enjoy. I have always expressed my preference
for simple lines and functionality. I use
simple materials in an honest way. I prefer
to leave things as they are and show how
they are made, letting nature take its course
and allowing the materials to express their
true texture and colour.

When I disconnect…

I am often at my vacation house in La Pedrera
in Uruguay. I really disconnect when I am
there with all my family. There is no wifi and
no television, so it's my time to connect with
myself, and I read a lot.

I have learnt to live without…

caring what people think about me.

I set boundaries around…

my design decisions. They are based on
modern and minimalist ideas – these are
the key areas of my work. I choose projects
that I'd like to be involved in and I prefer to
create more raw modern designs rather
than commercial ones.

Calm is…

when I have projects I like to do.

Change is…

something I'm always looking for.

When it comes to order and chaos
in my life…

I don't like chaos but sometimes it's exciting
because it helps to generate new ideas.

I care less about…

being famous.

I care more about…

thinking of new designs.

My life feels meaningful when…

I feel useful or I am finishing a project
that I really love.

What's most important in my life
right now is…

my health.

EMBRACING SLOW –
SUSTAINABLE, LOCAL, ORGANIC, WHOLE:

Sustainable living means…

mixing modern design with vintage classics.

Local is…

something I always try to support, such as
consuming local products.

Organic is…

something my wife Mercedes is passionate
about. She is always looking for organic food.
And we turn our food waste into compost to
use in the garden.

I feel Whole when…

we spend weekends at home – they are for
cooking with our kids and gardening. I also
enjoy working on wooden models, such as
planes or boats.

ANDREA MOORE

Meeniyan, Victoria, Australia

'When I am here I have time for reflection and observation. I feel calmer in less cluttered environments. I need space to think.'

For the past three years, Melbourne-based interior designer Andrea Moore has been transforming a group of disused dairy farm buildings into a retreat and a unique accommodation experience. Andrea's parents bought Ross Farm in 2005, a six-acre parcel of land in Meeniyan, near the southern tip of Victoria. Working alongside her father, Lindsay, a semi-retired veterinarian who has always been resourceful and enjoys working on passion projects – from cars to boats and houses – they are slowly bringing the old buildings back to life. This can-do attitude has been a defining feature of the Ross Farm project. 'Working with limited resources can be freeing in unexpected ways,' Andrea says. 'It has created opportunities to re-use materials that are already here. And we've tried to use them in interesting and unexpected ways, as well as make the most of elements such as light fittings, furniture and door hardware.'

Three buildings make up the Ross Farm project: The Cabin (the original 1960s house), which was finished a couple of years ago and, more recently, The Barn and The Dairy. Each property is self-contained and has its own private outlook. The father and daughter duo wanted to work within the buildings' footprints and utilise the existing structures as much as possible. 'It was too difficult to conform to the current building codes,' Andrea says. As a result, they mostly rebuilt them, cladding them in the existing materials while maintaining the original proportions where possible. They raised the roofline in The Barn to allow a mezzanine and added north-facing windows to capture the light and views of the surrounding South Gippsland hills.

The material palette of each building was inspired by the local landscape. In The Barn, Andrea used granite predominantly, inspired by nearby Wilsons Promontory National Park, which is known for its prehistoric landscape and granite boulders. It was used in the kitchen to form the cabinetry fronts and benchtop, in the bathroom from floor to ceiling, and as a continuous bench seat in the dining space.

Many of the materials for the project were sourced from the surrounding area too. A lot of the cypress timber used in construction, such as the framework for the sofa and butcher's block island in the kitchen, were milled locally. 'I have a strong idea of the overall aesthetic, which informs the design,' Andrea says. 'But it's led by the materials we can get. Everything is designed with that in mind. And in that way, it's been an organic process.'

As much as possible, they've used local suppliers and manufacturers. Andrea wanted to use rusted metal in the build and was inspired to create a spiral staircase. A company in the town of Leongatha folded corten steel for them, and then delivered the staircase to the site where Lindsay and local metalworker Paul Lovell assembled and installed it. 'We have been very lucky to work with a small group of talented local craftsmen who have a can-do approach to new ideas and working with different materials,' Andrea says.

Most of the project has been handcrafted, often at the hands of Lindsay and Paul, who work on site every day. 'Quite often I come up with an idea and we flesh it out as to how it can be resolved. That's when their skill set comes into play, because they have the fine solutions for achieving the result,' Andrea says. Building this way takes time, and Andrea admits it has provided several valuable lessons. 'You have to give in to the process,' she says. 'Sometimes you have your ideal design or end point but the process can actually make it better. I used to be a perfectionist but now I see more beauty in imperfection. As Dad often says, "It will take as long as it will take."'

Returning to the area where she grew up has provided Andrea a balm to the busyness of city life. 'When I come back to the country I instantly feel calmer and more grounded. Life is still busy, but I love the feeling of being more connected to nature and the seasons,' she says. 'The landscape is beautiful, we're surrounded by rolling hills and there are beautiful beaches just down the road. We are also lucky to have Wilsons Promontory National Park there on our doorstep – it's a slice of paradise.'

And now after years of hard work, Andrea is able to enjoy spending time in the kitchen that she designed and her dad built. 'That's where the handcrafted element comes in, because objects become full of meaning and that adds to the soul of the place,' she says. 'Everything has a story and this helps create its personality. Although I'm a minimalist, I'm not against having things for the sake of having them, but I'd rather they had purpose and meaning.'

When I do less…
I feel calmer – it gives me space to think more clearly. Quite often this is when new ideas start to flow.

When I disconnect…
it gives my mind space to be more creative. I like to take time to switch off from technology and be inspired by my surroundings.

I have learnt to live without…
unnecessary clutter. It's refreshing to pare back to basics and question what you really need and want to be surrounded by. Editing it down to things that you truly cherish.

I set boundaries around…
my personal time. I really value making time for family and friends, and I try to go for a surf every week. For me it's important to keep a healthy work–life balance.

Calm is…
for me, visiting the ocean. I always come away feeling calmer. There's nothing like the power of the waves to keep things in perspective.

Change is…
what you make of it. It can be cleansing to take a fresh look at your environment.

When it comes to order and chaos in my life…
I try to find the middle ground.

I care less about…
mainstream expectations. I'm more interested in forging my own path and creating my own story.

I care more about…
creating something authentic. I value the handcrafted and see beauty in imperfection and raw materials.

My life feels meaningful when…
I'm achieving my goals, whether it's professionally or personally.

What's most important in my life right now is…
being close to friends and family, living simply and making the most of every moment.

EMBRACING SLOW –
SUSTAINABLE, LOCAL, ORGANIC, WHOLE:

Sustainable living means…
living local, supporting local businesses and sharing produce within our small community.

Local is…
community. It's knowing your neighbours and helping each other out when needed.

Organic is…
being mindful. I really value learning the story and processes behind the handcrafted objects we bring into our home and daily life.

I feel Whole when…
my home is rich with meaning, and the unique objects that I have collected tell a story and are meaningful to me.

KASIA BILINSKI & MATTHEW MURPHY

Callicoon, New York, USA

'The property's sense of seclusion makes disconnecting and slowing down our tempo a natural instinct when we are at home. Living here feels Utopian – like nothing else exists, other than one another and the nature around us.'

After an unrelenting twelve years of working in the fashion and film industries, life changed 'overnight' for Kasia Bilinski and Matthew Murphy after the birth of their daughter, Thora, now aged four. 'Our priorities shifted completely,' Kasia says. 'We are still passionate about our jobs, but now we have to prioritise time for our family. We had never done that before. Living here has helped us with that shift.'

The couple met in Australia in 2004 when Matthew was living in Sydney; a few years later they moved to New York and lived in a series of one- and two-bedroom apartments. About a year after the birth of Thora, they decided to look for a place to retreat, somewhere that was within a two-hour commute of the city. On their first visit to Callicoon in Upstate New York, they were enchanted by the scenic drive, forests and rolling hills.

Although they knew very little about the area, they were intrigued by one of the properties they found. The home, hand-built by local carpenters and craftsmen in 1998, comprised three storeys and three bedrooms. It had an interesting post and beam construction and had been created from two separate barns from Pennsylvania, which had been dismantled and repurposed on a modern foundation. 'The story of the house grows each time we meet someone and learn another little part of its history,' Kasia says. Although someone had already made an offer on the house, the couple were persistent and eventually theirs was accepted when the other party failed to follow through.

After getting the keys in 2016, the couple lived in the house for a month before commencing any work. 'Things we initially considered must-dos became obsolete and other more meaningful ideas arose,' Kasia says. Living in the space gave them the idea to turn the ground floor wood workshop into the master bedroom, and dismantle the master bedroom on the top floor, turning it into a larger open space. A series of small rooms on the first floor were also opened up.

The first priority was to remove many of the internal walls and open up the main living area. They treated the rough pine walls by sanding and whitewashing, or 'pickling', them, as is said locally. Yellow pine floorboards were stained to tone down the oversaturated hues, and wood from the walls that had been removed in the living area was used to create the master bedroom on the ground floor.

The local neighbourhood is made up of a diverse range of people – from Brooklyn expats to artists and farmers, as well as young families seeking a quieter life. 'The thriving local community came as an unexpected surprise,' Kasia says. 'And it continues to surprise us in how quickly it is growing in such a positive way, one that feels true with our values and beliefs on how life should be led.'

However, adapting to a slower pace of life has taken some getting used to. 'People here operate on a different clock. We often jokingly say "country living" when someone takes a long time to get back to us on something,' Kasia says. 'Things aren't open twenty-four hours a day, so that forces you to plan ahead. And with careful planning, it's much easier to live more sustainably.' But it's a way of living that they both want Thora to experience. 'We feel that we've carved out a nice little corner of the world,' Matthew says.

Kasia and Matthew's fourteen-acre property extends over woodland and down to the edge of Callicoon Creek. The barn has a natural spring-fed pond full of salamander and koi, and they often see deer on the land, as well as mink and gophers. The chorus of bullfrogs is never far away, too. The garden, however, has required a lot of attention as vines had taken over large areas of the surrounding vegetation.

'There's always a little bit of magic here,' Kasia says. 'The other night there were fireflies down in the field. And even though it was past Thora's bedtime, it was just so incredible to see them.' Matthew agrees. 'The house is what got us here, but the property is why we stay.'

Kasia Bilinski & Matthew Murphy

When I do less…
I feel like I have taken the time to consciously pause, reflect and enjoy what is right in front of me. It's so easy to get wound up in the everyday, missing the most beautiful moments, or failing to see the importance of what we have.

When I disconnect…
I disconnect entirely. I get lost in the moment and for that moment nothing else exists.

I have learnt to live without…
mediocrity. If you are to put your efforts into something, pour your entire self into it. This was our philosophy with finding a home. It took us over five years because we didn't want to settle on something that wasn't right.

I set boundaries around…
things that become draining, whether it relates to work or people.

Calm is…
finding stillness, either for a brief moment or a longer period. I find calm through focusing myself on a project, from working in the yard to crafting a design by hand.

Change is…
often terrifying but needed in order to grow. A dear friend shared an excerpt from Osho that has really had an impact on me. It is based on the idea that what disappears from one side results in a resurrection on the other side.

When it comes to order and chaos in my life…
a property with so much nature around it has shown us how to balance our priorities, to know when to let things be as they want to be.

I care less about…
things that heighten my anxieties. Living here allows us to disconnect and manage stress that can arise while being in the city.

I care more about…
living lightly. We strive to minimise our impact on the environment – from what we eat to how we interact with our property and respect our surroundings.

My life feels meaningful when…
I see the impact of my efforts on others, including those within my community. We have supported and urged local businesses to be plastic and packaging free, and helped them with ideas on how to implement these practices.

What's most important in my life right now is…
providing a nourishing lifestyle for one another. We are striving to find a balance between cultural stimulation and an appreciation/mutual respect of nature and the environment.

**EMBRACING SLOW –
SUSTAINABLE, LOCAL, ORGANIC, WHOLE:**

Sustainable living means…
being considerate of the environment in all of our actions, no matter the scale. We strive to give back whatever we take and use only what we need. Nothing goes to waste in our home; there is always some use found for everything.

Local is…
supporting one another, living in symbiosis with our surroundings and being resourceful. Part of our transition to upstate life has been learning to work with what is available to us locally rather than seeking out imports. It often means compromise and a challenge, but when you see the positive impact it has on your surroundings it is rewarding in itself.

Organic is…
an appreciation of the raw elements in their purest form. Organic is undeliberate, by chance, and unpredictable. We seek out and admire the beauty of imperfection in our everyday lives, be it something we have created for the home ourselves by hand, a flawed apple picked off our tree or a cracked surface. We also consciously choose to eat organic foods from local farms.

I feel Whole when…
we are with one another and the ones we love, sharing a meal, appreciating the outdoors and the home we have created.

JESSICA KRAUS

San Clemente, California, USA

'There's a natural contentment here. We wanted to be by the water for so long. Everything we want is right here.'

After years of living tantalisingly close to the ocean but not being able to call it her home, Jessica Kraus made the move with her family of six in 2017. Even though they hadn't been that far from the beach – about an hour's drive from the Southern Californian coast – it was a significant step. Up until the summer of 2017 they had been living inland in a new-build home, and while she and her husband, Mike, had been busy over the years adding layers of interest, it didn't have the character that they were yearning for. The more the couple considered the move, the more they realised that what they also wanted to change was their lifestyle.

Life can get busy raising four young boys – Arlo, thirteen, Leon, ten, Rex, nine, and Hayes, five – and so, for them, the laid-back coastal community of San Clemente held lots of appeal. 'There's an old-school surf vibe here,' Jessica says. 'My kids don't have to wear shoes. And because the beach is the entertainment, it's easy to have four boys here. The community has really embraced them.'

Jessica was also attracted to the Spanish charm of the area. 'It's my favourite style of decor – old California,' she says. 'Everything that I gravitate towards is in that style.' The couple's first house was a 1927 Spanish bungalow, which was an apprenticeship of sorts for Mike, who has rebuilt or made modifications on all of their homes. Jessica, who had grown up watching her mother restore older houses over the years, realised she was missing the character of them when they began their search. 'I've always liked something with character, and things were made better then,' she says. 'We like old cars and old houses because they have such great inherent style.'

The couple found a 1960s ranch home that met their main criteria. 'We liked that we could afford it,' Jessica says. 'And we didn't even do an inspection report. It was close to the beach so we just said, "We'll take it." It looked nothing like it does now.'

The process of turning the house into a home has been slow. During the week Mike sets his alarm for 4.30 am to go to work and then returns at four in the afternoons to continue with the renovations, which extends into the weekends too. Each step of the way, he has learnt valuable skills that have helped make the next stage possible. The fireplace taught him how to work with plaster, which he then applied in the kitchen. Every improvement has been self-taught and perfected on the job.

The family moved into the house as soon as they got the keys. 'We slept on the floor,' Jessica says. 'It was so exciting to be here.' The first change was to tear down a wall in the kitchen area and open up the space to what had previously been bedrooms. They had always planned to remove the ceiling but weren't prepared for the feature beams that were hidden underneath. 'It was the best surprise,' Jessica says. There was another when they replaced a small bedroom window with a larger one in what is now the living area, and discovered they had ocean views.

Throughout the renovating process they have managed to stay within the building's original footprint – it remains a three-bedroom and two-bathroom home, albeit one that's been reconfigured. The upside is that they haven't had to worry about permits. Instead, the focus has been on creating a home that makes life easier and more enjoyable. Previously, the only access to the back deck was through the boys' bedroom but now its main entrance is off the kitchen. Mike has built closets where they can fit, and converted storage space in the boys' bedroom into bunk beds. And wherever Mike builds, Jessica is close behind, sourcing and requesting features such as porthole windows integrated within the bunk beds. However, they are careful not to make change just for change's sake. 'We want to honour that it's a 1960s ranch home,' Jessica says.

It is also important to create a hardy space. 'With everything we do, we ask ourselves if it can withstand four boys,' Jessica says. As a result, her choices have included waxed furniture so that handprints aren't visible, a low coffee table that's bulky and durable, and off-white tiles and grout. 'We choose things that already appear a little bit worn because they are going to end up that way, anyway,' she says. They are also conscious of staying within budget and prioritising sustainable choices. Most of the house has been fitted out with vintage or handmade pieces, the dining chairs were a street-side find, and the few new furniture pieces they did buy are American-made. One of the features of the home, a sideboard, was bought second-hand online.

Originally it was planned for the living room but didn't fit, and it was too big for the bathroom, so they built it into the kitchen. 'We liked it so much, we found a way to incorporate it somewhere else,' Jessica says.

The renovation continues at a slow pace, as time and money allow. The bedrooms and bathrooms are on the to-do list, as is extending the back deck. But first, the couple are hoping to build an onsite tiny house, which is traditionally a 160-square-foot (16-square-metre) space, that they can rent out.

While some areas of the home are in flux, Jessica creates calm in what remains. 'I like a sparse decor because I feel there is so much chaos in our life, which is part of being in a big family,' she says. 'I like simple living. Aesthetics are important to me, and I try to go with minimal, easy pieces. But I like to slowly gather only what I like.'

As for Mike, he's pushing to get the work done. 'He wants to finish it and hang out and go surfing on the weekends,' Jessica says. But for now, he has to speed up so he can slow down.

When I do less…
I feel more at ease in my surroundings. I enjoy
a slow frameless day without hours stacked
by schedule.

When I disconnect…
I feel a sense of relief. Constant connection can
feel like an overload at times, so it's always so
nice to see how quickly you forget about
all of that when you make a conscious effort
to disconnect.

I have learnt to live without…
needless want. The older I get the less I want.

I set boundaries around…
my free time, my hobbies, my morning routine.

Calm is…
a state I am constantly seeking but rarely
achieve. There's a lot going on with four boys.
Calm, in literal terms, rarely finds us here.

Change is…
harder than it used to be.

When it comes to order and chaos
in my life…
I try my best to embrace both ends of it.
You have to with children.

I care less about…
status. Things like what you do, where you
come from. I prefer to be surrounded by
genuinely real, unpolished people at ease
in their own skin.

I care more about…
getting this house done.

My life feels meaningful when…
my children are inspired.

What's most important in my life
right now is…
fostering a nurturing home environment
for our family.

**EMBRACING SLOW –
SUSTAINABLE, LOCAL, ORGANIC, WHOLE:**

Sustainable living means…
thrifted goods, handmade furniture,
smarter consumption.

Local is…
important. Establishing roots in community
is our responsibility. Caring for the kids in
the neighbourhood, being involved in small
politics, school functions – all the facets that
lend to public enrichment.

Organic is…
anything that is uniquely, mindfully
constructed.

I feel Whole when…
I am keenly present and invested in the
things I love.

THE SLOW RENOVATION

There is a lot to be gained from patience and perseverance – often more than we expect. Writer Jessica Kraus shares the lessons she has learnt over the past couple of years while slowly creating a home with her husband, Mike, for their family of six in Southern California.

Jessica Kraus

As a young couple we used to dream about moving to San Clemente, a small sleepy surf town notorious for its old-school longboarding vibes. We had always been drawn to this place, littered with taco stands and sun-bleached Volkswagen vans parked along ragged suburban streets lined with a mix of quirky, old Spanish bungalows, wood-shingled cottages and mid-century housing tracts. Living here was a fantasy we saw dissolve in recent years, though, due to soaring coastal real estate prices and cash investors edging us out of the market.

We had all but given up on finding a house we could actually afford here when Mike came across an ad for a house for sale on Craigslist in the summer of 2017. It was a run-down 1964 ranch-style house that had too many issues to count, but it was well under market value and, in many ways, felt like a 'last chance' for us. Before we knew it we were packing up our inland tract home and moving into a house half the size, a mile from the beach.

The two years following have been consumed by a whole house restoration, reimagining the space so that the layout better suited our family of six. This meant drafting a fresh vision for a house lacking what I typically love best about old homes: good bones and character. This one didn't have the kind of original features worth preserving, but it granted us the freedom to work from scratch in revising things with an equal emphasis on both the practical and aesthetic aspects of design. Comfort, flow and function were the top priorities as we sought to make smarter use of every inch of the 1650 square feet (153 square metres) available.

Anything that felt unnecessary was eliminated entirely. Walkways were opened up, unused doorways were closed over, ceilings taken out and bunks built into existing closet spaces in smaller rooms to free up floor space. Taking the ceiling out offered additional height, which made the whole house feel much lighter and more open, as did moving the kitchen to the opposite end of the house, so that the common living area now framed our slice of blue harbour view.

None of this has come fast or easy for us. Mike, being the sole constructor here, has managed the logistics and contributed his own labour within his limited hours after work and on weekends, in between the regular things that come with raising kids. Tackling one wall demolition and plumbing catastrophe at a time...

The whole renovation process proved a far cry from the trigger-quick 'before and afters' seen on home improvement TV shows. While these shows tout painless and immediate transformations, our experience was the exact opposite. Some months we felt like we were camping. Without a working heater or cosy bedrooms to hide away in, without designated spaces for our things or pretty places to arrange, carving out pockets of peace amidst the chaos became a new working skill for each of us. The inconveniences of crumbling walls and endless sawdust, blaring power tools and piles of debris scattered everywhere can really get to you. But in hindsight, it serves as a testament to patience.

Having to live alongside this renovation showed us just how much we can adapt and thrive when forced to. It also garnered a richer sense of pride in what we've accomplished. Because every end result came slow and hard, there's not an inch of it that I dare take for granted.

Having to condense square footage also served as the motivating factor to do what we've always wanted: simplify our life. It forced us to pare down belongings and focus on being outdoors as much as possible with four growing boys. Living close to the ocean inspires an innate sense of contentment, which seems to eclipse the need for 'things'. I find myself wanting and needing less since moving here. Free time is devoted to all that our surroundings have to offer – surfing, picnics on the sand, bonfires, bike riding and, of course, the tireless thrill of watching the sun sink into the ocean from a rocky stoop at the jetty.

One of my favourite pastimes these days is driving around town on foggy mornings on my way to grab coffee, admiring what remains of the original beach cottages scattered along the hillsides on the PCH (Pacific Coast Highway). I love imagining which homes could be saved or restored, who lived there and what the town was like when the house was built. It pains me to see some of my favourite houses torn down and replaced by the towering soulless mansions funded by investors who will likely never live there. It makes me question why there aren't more laws to preserve the laid-back appeal SoCal so perfectly forged here in its young formative days. These old homes are part of our town's backstory – what a shame to erase the humble beauty so inherit in them.

But I'm hopeful that the trend for smaller houses and slower living will continue to gain speed and encourage people to embrace the allure of simplicity in how they approach views on modern housing. I applaud the kind of cultural awakening that embraces owning and wanting less, and hope that our children, as they grow, might appreciate how liberating that can be. A bigger house doesn't always mean better living. And if you work hard enough at the things you yearn for, they just might reward you in big, messy, wild ways.

In the meantime, we're just happy to have all the dust and destruction mostly behind us. Now we can enjoy being parked on the sand all summer long, and then coming home in the evenings and collapsing inside these warm, welcoming walls we worked hard, and waited so long, for.

Writing is a unifying thread throughout the life of **JESSICA KRAUS**. After graduating from California State University with a BA in Creative Writing, she has carved out a space of her own in the online world with House Inhabit, an award-winning blog where she documents her life experiences while childrearing and undertaking renovations.

'The real voyage of discovery consists not in seeking new lands but seeing with new eyes.'

Marcel Proust

NOW

We live in a time of great freedom, but also high expectations. This age of choice can be both liberating and paralysing. In the past, our identity was something that was assigned to us – we were defined by where we were born, our parents and their social standing, and our trade, employment or business. We had no choice but to live and work on the family farm or continue the trade of our parents. Our community also defined us and created a sense of belonging. It provided a calendar of rituals that would mark our lives from the day we were born until our death. We had to maintain the social codes of the group or face ostracism, a harsh punishment for social creatures. Definitions of self and key life decisions were predetermined. Today, in a secularised world, we have both the freedom and burden to define our own identity. We can live almost anywhere we choose – from the suburbs of the city to a small country village. And with that often comes anxiety. Is this the right decision? Is this a good choice?

Technology has increased the possibilities of where we can live too. There are now places all over the world that are benefiting from a growing creative economy that has been fuelled by high-speed internet and advances in e-commerce and a multitude of software programs. Zones along both the east and west coasts of the USA and northern New South Wales region of Australia are just a few areas that offer an enticing alternative to traditional suburban life for the likes of digital nomads and a newly defined creative class who work in technology, design, media and the arts. All over the world, smaller cities and their outlying areas – generally within a two- to three-hour drive of the city – are undergoing renewal too; people don't always have to live in the capitals anymore. These areas hold great appeal for those who want to tap into city life when needed, but enjoy the benefits of being surrounded by natural scenery for the rest of their days.

However, while there are times when we crave change, other times that's what we fear. We often oscillate between order and chaos in our lives. The appeal of another place can be strong, though. We can feel the pull when we are on a holiday. We start imagining how our lives might improve in a different environment. The idea of escape is tantalising. And while we may be better suited to some communities with more like-minded people, moving homes is not a cure-all. As Ernest Hemingway wrote in *The Sun Also Rises*, we can't get away from ourselves by moving from one area to another. Whether it's changing cities or countries, it is easy to hope that all of our problems and concerns will be left behind. But wherever we are, so are they.

In a similar way, we can bestow expectations upon a home. We imagine that a new place might improve our lives. And while some changes at home come with benefits, they alone cannot guarantee contentment. Yet we often hope that tomorrow's dwelling will solve today's problems.

But what if there was a way to appreciate what we already have? What if it was a simple idea that merely required us to be present in the moment? One of the easiest ways to enjoy our life is to live mindfully. When we live in the now, we start to see the beauty of what is right in front of us. We stop looking over there and projecting, and wishing to be someplace else. We start to realise that no product can fill a need. Being present is one of the biggest challenges to consumerism – because instead of wanting, we start engaging and appreciating our lives in deeper and more meaningful ways. We can feel more connected to our home, community and environment too. We learn that we already have everything we need.

LET GO

One of the most powerful antidotes to consumerism is to let go of our attachment to objects. Buddhism refers to greed as the leading poison of the mind. It is an impulse to acquire what we desire in the belief it will make us happy. This can be everything from wanting bigger homes to more stuff than we can name. It is an element of our lives that continues to be out of balance. And it doesn't just relate to what we fill our homes with, but the speed at which we live our lives too.

What do we fear? Do we see having less as a sign of failure? Are we worried that slowing down is for underachievers? Is there some deep-rooted belief that if we don't meet all of our desires and push ourselves to the point of exhaustion in the process that we won't get anywhere in life, or amount to anything? However, when we let go of our attachment to objects and certain ideas, we create more time and space for what matters most. But know that in growth there is almost always loss, which is necessary to open the way for more of the life we want.

SWITCH OFF

What does the deluge of information overload we are exposed to on a daily basis add to our lives? Does it improve them in any meaningful way? Does it make us feel less tired, stressed or overwhelmed? Often the messages we receive are just another way to sell a product or service. And it is easy to become distracted with other people's choices. Comparison has become one of the most traded human currencies. It has become the driving force behind so many decisions and purchases. But comparison also deprives us of joy.

In a time when most of our day-to-day connections are made via devices, human connection has never been so important. We are social beings; we need to experience eye contact and touch. Nothing beats community in real life. When we disconnect from technology, we can reconnect with what brings true joy and contentment. And there are some things that can't be shared online: a cup of tea, a slice of cake, a glass of wine, an engaged conversation. The good stuff in life.

LIVE IN THE NOW

We can experience calm and a sense of stillness at home when we live in the present moment. One of the simplest ways to access this is through mindfulness, a form of meditation. It costs no money or time but requires our attention. It awakens us to the real beauty of our lives. We can practise it while standing in the shower or making a morning coffee. It begins with awareness, which we can cultivate through paying attention in a sustained and consistent way. The aim is to focus on being in the moment; otherwise, we are always moving through moments in the hope that the next one will be better.

It is also a way to let go of the noise of the mind – our ego. When we practise mindfulness we come to realise that we are not our thoughts; they are just thoughts. It is a way we can counter the chatter that encourages us to consume and want more; the self-talk that compares our lives and homes to those of others. Jon Kabat-Zinn, a scientist who has been championing the benefits of mindfulness for more than forty years, says it's a simple way to let go and engage in non-striving. It is a way we can pay attention to what matters most in our life, and engage in it more fully. When we live in the moment we can experience more inner peace and contentment too.

CULTIVATE GOOD FEELINGS

We invest a lot of hope in our homes. We want them to be the best expression of ourselves. So how do we decide what is necessary and what is based on greed or vanity? And how can we steer away from what is wasteful? How can we strike a balance between meeting our needs and wants? Within our own family we might have to decide between a bigger house or family holidays, a renovation or school fees. Or maybe we want to take a lower income to spend more time at home with young children. And what about our contributions to the wider community and the world at large – is there a way to be an engaged member of a family and also be of service to others beyond the home? Should we consider if there are more worthy ways to spend our hard-earned money? When there are so many who have so little, how can we shift our focus away from materiality? And when we are already busy, *how* can we find the time to work out our priorities? It is when we slow down that we can make more informed decisions about what feels right. We can act rather than react.

When we live mindfully we become more aware of when we feel at our best, too. This can be in many areas of our life – from the food we eat to the people we meet, as well as movement and meditation. We can also pay attention to how our home makes us feel. Do we prefer to live in a tidy space with less stuff, for example? Let's follow our curiosity and see if it leads to what we're passionate about. Focus on that too.

Carl Honoré, in his seminal book *In Praise of Slow*, encourages everyone to find their *tempo giusto* – their right speed; sometimes fast, sometimes slow but always with a focus on being present and prioritising quality over quantity. He says the central idea behind the slow movement is to do things well, enjoying the process more. This approach to life supports good health in our bodies and minds, as well as in our relationships, communities and the environment. It doesn't claim to be a one-size-fits-all approach. Instead, it encourages everyone to find their *eigenzeit*, or 'own time'. Every person, event, project or moment has its own inherent pace.

COURTNEY ADAMO

Bangalow, New South Wales, Australia

'We knew that we'd embraced a slower life when we realised there was nowhere else we'd rather be and had accepted that everything we had in our life was enough.'

For almost two years Courtney Adamo travelled around the world with her family of six in search of a slower way of life. After moving from the USA with husband Michael and living in London for twelve years, they decided to pack up again and take a family gap year, hoping to find somewhere slower to live with their four children, Easton, now fourteen, Quin, twelve, Ivy, ten, and Marlow, seven. They found the life they had been seeking in the hills above Byron Bay in Australia, and have since welcomed their fifth child, Wilkie, two.

The Adamos were drawn to the area for many reasons – its natural beauty, the climate, beaches and access to good food – but it was the creative community that held the biggest appeal. 'There is a general like-mindedness of the people who live in this region, with priorities being placed on the environment, local and organic food, as well as a healthy lifestyle, and more,' Courtney says. 'Because there aren't a lot of big industries in the region, apart from tourism, many of the people living here have to go back to doing what they're passionate about, and that means you get lots of people with creative jobs, many of whom are happy to support each other. It's a very collaborative, creative community.'

Courtney says it's almost impossible to compare the Byron community to the friends they had in the UK. 'London is like any big city in that you have lots of people in high-profile jobs, working long hours, with lots of stress. People are busy,' she says. 'London is also such a transient city. People come and go so often that you never feel comfortable getting too close to anyone because you know that they'll most likely leave at some point. In the twelve years we lived there, seven good friends left. Easton also lost several of his best friends: one moved back to America, one to Amsterdam, and two different friends moved to Paris. There's something about London that just doesn't feel permanent, and in a way that hardens you to forming new friendships.'

The couple's priorities have also realigned. Life is less expensive than in London, so they don't face the same financial pressures as before. 'We aren't as concerned about climbing the corporate ladder, achieving important titles or earning more money,' Courtney says. 'We are content with making enough money to live comfortably, eat well, surf often and travel occasionally.'

The rhythm of life has also changed considerably. 'In London, there was always something new and exciting to do – a new museum exhibit, a new restaurant to try, a show to see,' Courtney says. 'Our options for things to do on a weekend were endless, which of course we loved, but it did keep us busy. Here, there are fewer things to do and they all involve being outside and in nature. So we often end up at the beach, repeating what we did the weekend before. It's a good thing we all really love surfing, because no one complains about this simple weekend ritual.'

The family spend most of their time outdoors, so living in a much smaller home compared with their five-bedroom London townhouse isn't an issue. The couple bought a three-bedroom cottage in the small country town of Bangalow in May 2018 after househunting for more than six months. 'We were hoping to buy a house on a bit of land, with views of the sunset and rolling green hills,' Courtney says. 'But when I walked into this house for the first time, I just knew it was our home.'

When the couple renovated the house, they kept mostly within the building's footprint, reconfiguring some of the rooms to make the place more liveable. The site of the bathroom and kitchen were swapped to create a better inside–outside flow, and to allow the dining room to open off the kitchen so that area would function better as a communal space. They also converted a sunroom into a small bedroom for Wilkie. 'One of my favourite things about this home is that we literally use every square inch of space,' Courtney says. 'There is no room in the house that doesn't get used every single day.'

They gave as much consideration to what they retained as what they left out. 'It was important not to change the character of the home or wipe it clean of the charm and original features,' Courtney says. They retained the original wooden arch between the lounge and dining rooms, and kept the old floors, creaky windows and doors with clunky doorknobs.

One of the big lessons Courtney and Michael learnt while travelling around the world was how little they needed – on a practical everyday living level as well as experientially. 'I'm conscious of not having too much stuff in the house because it can easily become overwhelming,' she says. As storage space is limited, they ensure that everything they own gets used regularly. This minimalist approach extends to their goal of living a simpler and more meaningful life and to creating a space in which their children feel safe, comfortable and happy. 'I want my kids to have so many happy memories of their childhood in our home,' Courtney says. 'I love that we have a space where we can enjoy being together – often cooking in the kitchen or sitting around our dining table enjoying a meal.'

When the family left London, Courtney said they wanted to find 'somewhere slower' to live. After eighteen months of travel through fifteen countries in North and South America, Europe, New Zealand, Asia and Australia, they found it in a small and sleepy country town near Byron Bay.

Courtney Adamo

When I do less…
I have mixed feelings. I'm happy doing less if I know I've already been busy doing everything I need to do. If I have a lot on my to-do list, it's not easy for me to switch off from that. Equally, I don't mind having a lot to do – it gives me purpose. It's about finding the balance.

When I disconnect…
I feel much more present and in tune with myself and my family.

I have learnt to live without…
my extended family. It may seem like a funny thing to say, but Michael and I have now lived far away from our families for sixteen years. While we miss them terribly, we also love where we live, and thankfully there is FaceTime.

I set boundaries around…
screen time. We have made the decision not to have a TV, and to keep the kids from owning or using electronic games or devices. While we let them watch the occasional film, it's a rare treat and not a norm.

Calm is…
being out in the ocean on my surfboard, watching and waiting for waves.

Change is…
a good thing! All the big changes in my life have always led to something wonderful.

When it comes to order and chaos in my life…
I have both in equal measure.

I care less about…
what other people think of me. For me, this has been one of the benefits of growing older. It seems the older I get, the less concerned I've become with impressing other people, and the more natural it feels to simply be me.

I care more about…
raising children who are kind, compassionate and as interested as they are interesting.

My life feels meaningful when…
I'm in the car with my family. I don't know what it is about being in the passenger seat – Michael driving, the kids in the back, music playing – that makes me feel so present and reflective. It feels a huge responsibility having a car full of children, and it always gives me such a sense of purpose.

What's most important in my life right now is…
health, happiness and surfing.

EMBRACING SLOW –
SUSTAINABLE, LOCAL, ORGANIC, WHOLE:

Sustainable living means…
doing everything you can, even little things, to reduce your footprint on this planet. It's about acknowledging that we are all living on a land with limited resources and we need to be conscious about what we consume.

Local is…
always our first choice. Thankfully we live in a wonderful area with so many local brands, businesses and people we are happy to support.

Organic is…
better for our bodies and for the planet. Again, I'm thankful to live in a place that values an organic lifestyle – from the food we eat and the clothes we wear, to the products we use on our bodies and in our homes, there are so many great options available to us.

I feel Whole when…
everything feels balanced, but it has to feel like the right mix of work, play, family and friends. I suppose it's the feeling of a sunny, unscheduled weekend after a busy, productive week. When all the work is done and I get to be with my family and friends at the beach – that's when I feel whole.

LETTING GO

When Courtney Adamo, an entrepreneur in the family lifestyle arena, decided to take a gap year to travel the world with her family, she faced many big changes. First, she decided to sell the London home she had lovingly renovated a few years earlier to fund the trip. Then she sold off many of her family's possessions to lighten their load. Finally, she said goodbye to cherished friends and a school community that she revered. But while letting go often makes others come unstuck, Courtney soon realised she had an entirely different approach.

Courtney Adamo

The question wasn't one I was expecting. Why have I always found it so easy to let go? But it wasn't just one question, it was many – all variations on the same theme. Why was it easy for me to leave America and move to London with my new boyfriend back in 2003? After twelve years in London, how were we able to leave behind the life we knew, sell a house we had recently renovated, and part with our treasured belongings to set off on our round-the-world travels in 2015? How were we able to start all over again when we moved to Australia in 2016?

I sat on these questions for a few months, reminiscing on the roads that have led me here and the many turns we've eagerly taken, pondering that question of *why*. And the truth is that I still don't have an answer. I guess I find it equally puzzling why some people *can't* let go. The idea of being so laden with attachment, so anchored to one place, makes me feel as uncomfortable as I imagine one might feel about my ability to let go so easily.

One afternoon in London, when we were preparing for our big adventure, one of the mums at my children's school approached me. She had heard about our plans to sell the house and shed our belongings and broached the topic with an expression of worry I will never forget. 'But what happens when you come back? What if you can't find a home as nice as yours? Won't you miss your favourite furniture? How will you ever get your kids back in to this school? What happens if you get really sick while you're travelling? What if something goes wrong while you're away?'

I'm pretty sure the look on my face is one she will never forget either. I honestly hadn't even considered any of those potential problems. I didn't even know what to say in reply to all of her questions. In fact, I stood there speechless, unable to answer. We both looked at each other in utmost confusion, like two different species of human: one who was eagerly and excitedly planning a life change without any fears for the future, and another who was so consumed by the potential pitfalls of our plans that her concern was unmistakable. She later confided, as we walked back to our cars, that she only wished she could be as brave. That's really when it dawned on me that what we were doing was actually *adventurous*.

Up until then, I hadn't considered that our plans involved risk. We had excitedly decided to spend a year travelling with our children. I was so focused on this upcoming year of travel and togetherness, I didn't have the capacity to worry about life *after* our adventure. And, in all honesty, it didn't feel like we were letting go; it felt like we were on the cusp of something amazing and exciting. However, as I drove home that afternoon, I began to doubt myself. Was I being careless? Should I be more upset about selling our home and more concerned for our future? Was I completely heartless for not being more emotionally attached to our belongings?

Over the next few weeks we made countless trips to the charity shop, we donated toys and clothes to friends, and we sold most of our bigger furniture pieces online. Gradually our possessions were removed from the house, one by one. I found it surprisingly easy to let these pieces go. It felt liberating to become untethered, and I felt lighter and freer with each letting go.

And then one day a woman came to pick up the two Stokke highchairs we'd listed for sale online. We'd bought one of the highchairs in 2005 for Easton when he was a baby and the other for Quin when he was born. As I helped carry the chairs out to her car, I felt a lump in my throat start to form and my arms started shaking. Suddenly, ten years of memories started flooding into my head: Michael feeding Easton his first bite of solids in a tiny flat in Notting Hill, Quin as a baby eating a punnet of raspberries at the table near the window, the two boys sitting side by side in our flat in Hampstead, birthday parties, holidays, special moments spent at the dining table with our children. It was like a scene in a movie where a hundred memories flash in the span of a minute. I set the highchairs in the boot of the woman's car, waved goodbye as she drove off, and walked back across the road with tears rolling down my cheeks.

I wasn't heartless after all; the tears were proof. But, of course, it wasn't the chairs I was attached to, it was the memories and milestones they symbolised. As I walked back into our home, I had a sudden sense of feeling peaceful and free – that I could let go of stuff knowing that I would always be able to hold on to what was most important. With twelve years of happy memories behind me and a future utterly unknown, I felt completely at ease in the space in between.

That's the thing about letting go: it allows you to acknowledge where and how you stand in the present moment, untethered from the past and empowered for the future.

COURTNEY ADAMO, a mother of five, has been a writer and entrepreneur for more than a decade. She is co-founder of the parenting website Babyccino and co-author of the book *9 Months*. Most recently she created an online community, The Loop, as a way for parents to connect, share and learn from each other.

AMEÉ & GLEN ALLSOP

East Hampton, New York, USA

'Living here has helped us feel grateful for what we have. As soon as we stop and look around and appreciate our present circumstance, the struggle to keep up with anyone else fades.'

After living in New York City for almost a decade, Ameé and Glen Allsop were ready for a change of scene. An idea on where they might live started to form a few years ago after Ameé, an architect, had worked on a project in Amagansett on Long Island. 'I liked that the area was still close to the city and it had a great history to it – many artists, writers and designers have lived here,' she says. 'We were starting to crave more headspace, nature, the ocean, and then wanting to grow our family. Not that you can't have kids in the city, but for us it was good to have some space.'

'We tend to change when we need to,' says Glen, a photographer. 'Deep down we thought it would be nice to have a house out of the city. In New York it's good to have an outside escape where there are less people in your face. For us, it was all about having farmers' stands, great food and fresh air.'

The move was made easier because of Ameé and Glen's type of work. 'We are super grateful that we don't have to be in the city from a client work point of view. A lot of our friends would love to move but they have desk jobs,' he says. Glen travels into the city about once a week for work, often booking back-to-back meetings to make the most efficient use of his time. 'It's a crazy day, but it's so effective,' he says. 'And even though it's a two-and-a-half hour drive, it used to take me an hour to travel just from Brooklyn to Manhattan.'

Creating both mental and physical space was an important factor for both of them. 'I wanted somewhere away from the hustle of the city so I could think straight again. While city living can be good in a certain season of your life, it was time to create more space for creativity,' Glen says. 'Although there are benefits of living in the city, it can be hard to carve out the time to nurture your own artistic voice and work.' Since the move he has been focused on creating a range of photographic prints, while Ameé has designed her first furniture collection, inspired by the idea of quiet living. 'Here we can be more intentional about the type of work we want to do,' Glen says. 'We're not necessarily slowing down but just cutting the noise.'

The couple started to look at homes in the Hamptons area about three years ago. After an exhaustive search, they narrowed the list down to eight houses to view. 'It was the last one on the last day and that was it – done,' Glen says. At the end of a long, curved driveway they found an early 1980s barn-shaped house covered with cedar shingles. 'Everyone thought we'd want something that we could renovate, but Ameé knew how much work a renovation would be, so we were more interested in something with good bones,' Glen says. 'Open living is hard to find. And this had the right amount of character without needing a ton of work.'

The house, which is only eight minutes' drive from the nearest beach and harbour, is on a one-acre block of land that backs onto a reserve – with not a neighbour in sight. The property provides the space they were craving, plus it gives five-year-old son Navy more freedom. 'The first weekend he was wandering around the whole property – it's such a nice space for him,' Glen says. 'He couldn't do that in the city. And there's a certain satisfaction with being in nature.' Now the family has baby Finn, who will be able to enjoy the surrounds in due time, too.

And while everyone asks them when they are going to make some changes to the house, the couple say they're not in a rush. It was a year before they painted the floors downstairs and another six months before changing an avocado-green wall in their bedroom to white. They have since neutralised a navy-blue guest bedroom, yellow kitchen and second bedroom, and the merlot hallway and stairwell. 'What you think you will do changes the longer you are in the house,' Ameé says. 'Everyone is expecting us to do something substantial, but it's nice to wait.'

Since moving to the area, they have found many like-minds. 'We love that the community out here is a selection of New Yorkers who appreciate saltwater swims and fresh air,' Glen says. 'Most of them have lived for a period of time in the city, so there's a common history and an intentionality to moving east, which automatically brings people together, no matter what age you are.'

They have also come to realise that living without conveniences can sometimes be beneficial. 'Not having everything at our doorstep has forced us to slow down in a good way, because it means we don't have everything knocking at our door both figuratively and physically,' Ameé says. 'While we miss walking downstairs to the coffee shop, it's a nice feeling being intentional about being at home or being out. We feel less anxiety when we decide to stay home, because even when we're home we can enjoy being outside. This line was often blurred when living in Brooklyn.'

The flip side to the lack of cafe convenience is that they regularly visit farmers' stands for food supplies. 'It's been a revelation eating fruit and vegetables that are in season,' Ameé says. 'It's a nice reality check when only certain foods are available due to weather or the time of year.' They feel more connected to nature in other ways too. Their water supply is from a well and not mainline, which has made them reflect more on what goes into the soil and eventually down into the water table. As a result, they are more conscious of using products without chemicals and toxins.

This a place where they can experience all four seasons, too. In summer they go down to the beach every morning as part of their routine. 'We forget about the rest of the world,' Ameé says. And in winter they take nature walks in Montauk or visit a nearby frozen pond. 'When it snows, it's so magical here,' she says. 'We are so close to everything and yet we feel we are in the middle of nowhere,' Glen says.

Ameé & Glen Allsop

When I do less…
I feel more focused.

When I disconnect…
I connect with the present and leave the past
and future in the background.

I have learnt to live without…
home delivery. It was a tough transition but,
hey, we're better off without it.

I set boundaries around…
screen time for our five-year-old. We're not
anti-screens but we definitely want him to
engage with physical things around him,
whether it's Lego, a puzzle, conversation
or the beach.

Calm is…
a morning walk along the beach when the
ocean is glass and the temperature is just right.

Change is…
inevitable. Certain baselines will never change,
such as 'this is our family', but anything else
is adaptable.

When it comes to order and chaos
in my life…
chaos is always going to be temporary,
so that's okay.

I care less about…
other people's opinions and more about
whether or not what and where and how
we are going about something is truly the
direction that we should be heading in.
We follow our own hearts and so long as we
are on the same page together we know that
we're good.

I care more about…
the quality of life for our kids.

My life feels meaningful when…
Navy is running along the shoreline on a
Wednesday afternoon at 3 pm in complete
happiness and contentment, amazed by
the waves chasing his toes. It's so simple,
but all of our major life decisions – from
career paths, moving to New York and then
out here – make sense when we see how
naturally happy he is here.

What's most important in my life
right now is…
to shake off any external pressures to be or
do anything else apart from first and foremost
caring for and loving Finn, a new little life
who has been entrusted to us.

**EMBRACING SLOW –
SUSTAINABLE, LOCAL, ORGANIC, WHOLE:**

Sustainable living means…
no anxiety about 'tomorrow'. Slow living
means each step is intentional, there's no rush
in getting there because the pace needs to be
sustainable. It's a long journey, not a sprint.

Local is…
a swim in the ocean and then grabbing a loaf
of bread from Carissa's and swinging by
the farm stand on the way home for a few
bits and pieces.

Organic is…
Is this us? Is this natural for us? Is it easy?
Does it feel right? It could relate to friends,
new clients or a project. If it's organic, it
will slide right in like it was always there.

I feel Whole when…
there's a good rhythm – working with great
clients, producing meaningful work and being
present with friends and family when we are
not in work mode.

CHARLOTTE MINCH

Tisvildeleje, Denmark

'Every day I go into the garden and pick flowers, or ride my bicycle through the woods. This is where I come to relax.'

Tisvildeleje is a small historic village on the north coast of Denmark, known for its sweeping beaches and soft sand dunes. The town sits on a stretch of coastline known as the Danish Riviera, and is a popular summer destination for both families and couples. Although the thatched-roof cottages that overlook the ocean are some of the most popular in the area, Charlotte Minch wanted to find a weekend getaway that was away from the beach, somewhere more private and tucked away from the crowds.

For most of the week Charlotte, an interior designer, lives in Copenhagen with her husband, Pedro Heyman, a retired fruit merchant, in an apartment near the water. But about two years ago she realised she wanted to find somewhere to retreat, a place where she could feel surrounded by nature. 'I was looking for a garden where I could be by myself,' Charlotte says. 'I like privacy and to feel that I'm hiding away.' She was attracted to the area because it was near a beach and a wood. Plus, it's only a forty-minute drive from the city, making it an easy getaway.

'It's hard to find a place here,' Charlotte says. 'People often live in this area for many years. Houses are passed down from parents to children.' However, as it turns out, the place she found, which was built in 1858, had been for sale for a long time. 'It was too old,' she says. 'No one could see anything in it. They couldn't understand what to do, but I could see the vision, I could see it finished.'

'In theory, we shouldn't have bought it,' Charlotte says. 'It was not possible to live in it.' But because she enjoys bringing homes back to life, the couple took on the restoration. Consequently, Charlotte went to a museum in Denmark to see how buildings from that era were originally made. The ceiling had been closed in, so she opened it up but reinstalled the original beams to become a feature. 'They were so low you couldn't stand up,' she says. The *stråtag*

(thatched) roof had to be fixed too. 'It was expensive but it was a necessary cost,' she says.

Charlotte worked within the original footprint of the building, focusing on the interior spaces to make them feel more inviting. She converted the old barn into an ensuite for the master bedroom, and the kitchen was reconfigured with Charlotte's signature look of new materials made to look old. She stained oak cabinetry with black oil and added handles from the 1950s that were in a client's home. 'They were going to throw them out,' Charlotte says.

Kitchen shelves are filled with handmade black stone dinnerware from Colombia that Charlotte sells in her shop, Vivre Home. They are ovenproof and hardy. The zinc dining table sourced from India is also resilient. 'You can put anything on it, even if it's hot,' she says. 'You can put it in the rain too.'

And while the house features heirloom paintings, it feels far from austere. 'This is a summer house, so it can't be too precious,' Charlotte says. The mix of antiques with raw materials helps create a balance between beauty and practicality. Charlotte installed a Shaker-style peg rail around the perimeter of the kitchen to act as both a feature and a place to hang utensils, hats and clothes. Dark-coloured seating in the living room is forgiving for country living, and concrete floors are resilient to sand and dirt. Charlotte has been considered about all of her choices. 'In Denmark, summer homes often end up filled with odds and ends,' Charlotte says. 'People just put what they don't want at home, but I'm doing my job and creating a place where I want to be.'

Charlotte's summer home is enjoyed all year round. Winter is when the crowds are quiet and the couple take walks in the woods or have fireside chats. Charlotte and Pedro often arrive on a Friday evening and stay until Monday morning. They enjoy riding their bicycles down to the beach or going for a walk. Often neighbours pop over to say hello and stay for a glass of wine, or Charlotte rides into the village to buy fish and then cooks dinner for family and friends. This is when she relaxes, when she loses herself in the preparation of food and mealtimes. 'It's so nice to be here,' Charlotte says. 'I love the country life.'

When I do less…
I go into a state of dreaming. When I'm here,
I can really relax. I have a very busy life in
Copenhagen, but here I enjoy reading books
or listening to music.

When I disconnect…
I feel good. I put my phone away and feel
better for it.

I have learnt to live without…
most things. I have so many things in my
everyday business but I can live on a stone,
really. I like to live in nature. It might look
like I need it, but I don't need very much.
However, I do love having people around
me when I'm relaxing.

I set boundaries around…
nothing really. It's very important for me
not to be regimented. That's why I don't
get stressed with my job.

Calm is…
something that comes easily to me. My mum
was calm too. I always get the best out of
people because everyone has good inside of
them. Some people get angry and I can help
them to be calm.

Change is…
easy for me. I love change, but I also love to
take my old stuff with me so I feel at home.

When it comes to order and chaos
in my life…
I can handle chaos. I stay calm and say,
'we will get there'. I'm positive. Nothing
can get me down.

I care less about…
some of the people in the fashion industry.
I was a fashion designer before working
in interiors.

I care more about…
good health. We have always eaten well.
My mother was into vegetarian food years
ago, so it was normal for us. We are a healthy
family, and enjoy eating together.

My life feels meaningful when…
I have my family around me. My daughters
come and sleep on the weekend, and my
grandson enjoys visiting too.

What's most important in my life
right now is…
to be with my husband; he is the most
important thing. We have been together
since I was sixteen years old.

**EMBRACING SLOW –
SUSTAINABLE, LOCAL, ORGANIC, WHOLE:**

Sustainable living means…
buying from the farmers when I can. I enjoy
the seasonal food here, as it's so fresh.

Local is…
part of life in this village. There are a lot of
small shops that have everything. There's a
little restaurant and a small local supermarket.
Everyone says 'hello' and 'good morning'.
It's nice to have that sense of community.

Organic is…
something I embrace in my interiors.
I gravitate to natural materials. And all
of the kitchens I design are handcrafted.

I feel Whole when…
I find a way to access nature. Even when I'm
living in the city – and I love Copenhagen –
I will find a garden.

ROMI WEINBERG

Sydney, Australia

'I am most in the moment when I am cooking and sharing a meal at home with my family. I love hearing the girls play as I get creative in the kitchen, and the conversations we share over a meal.'

A short walk from the water and moored boats of one of Sydney's inner harbourside suburbs is a house hidden from view. 'It can't be seen from the street, which really appeals to me,' says owner Romi Weinberg. 'The house already felt like a sanctuary when I bought it. And it was this element that attracted me to it the most.'

Romi bought the house about three years ago as a fresh start. 'I find it exciting to have a new project,' she says. 'It was fun to consider the possibilities of a new space, and I loved everything about the creative process.' In her previous home she had engaged her sister, an interior designer, to guide the project. 'I didn't think I could do it myself,' explains Romi, who studied and worked in fashion. But this time she took on the challenge.

Family is a fundamental part of Romi's life. The rhythm of her days is based on the movements of her two daughters, Bo, twelve, and Tatum, seven, and nurturing their needs. But beyond her self-contained unit, she is also part of her own extended family. Daily phone calls with her mother are a thread that weaves itself through her week. And her sister is never far away. Often they all come together, including her father and nephews, at Romi's home on a Friday evening to celebrate Shabbat, the Jewish day of rest. 'It is a beautiful custom and I love hosting it at my place,' Romi says.

Romi had known about the house for many years because her parents were close friends with the original owners. 'It was always a favourite of mine,' she says. 'Being tucked away from the street, it felt like a little private oasis.' Romi bought the house within five days of it going onto the market. 'It was a no-brainer,' she says. 'I knew it was special and perfect for the girls and me.'

While the house had beautiful character, Romi wanted to adapt some of the French and Italian detailing to give the home a more contemporary Mediterranean feel. The mustard exterior was painted white and a simplified colour palette was continued throughout the interior. Tiles and carpets were removed and pine floorboards were laid and painted white. She also used a Moroccan plaster finish called *tadelakt* throughout the bedrooms and kitchen. All new joinery was coated in it, as well as some walls and flooring.

The heart of the house, the kitchen, underwent the biggest change. 'The existing space was too small for me,' Romi says. 'I'm very passionate about cooking. Entertaining family and friends is a regular part of our lives, so having a large, central kitchen was very important.' To extend the entertaining area, Romi added an undercover space outside constructed of old timber latte sticks. And because the pantry was quite small, she created a larger walk-in cupboard under the stairs, to store her extensive collection of chopping boards and catering provisions.

'I didn't want to change the overall footprint of the house because it was perfect as is,' Romi says. She retained the pool and outside area and only cosmetic changes were made to the spaces upstairs. Her previous home was much more contemporary in design. 'Both houses used white as the foundation, but this place has a much softer feeling. I find a neutral palette relaxing and calming – I love the cleanliness and purity of it,' she says.

To add warmth and character, Romi layered the house with textural elements such as weathered timber, woven baskets and large Moroccan rugs, as well as antique and vintage items. 'I love having beautiful objects around me,' she says. 'I look at them constantly and appreciate how they make me feel. It's also important for me to have a tidy, clean and organised home. I can't function in mess. I prefer everything to have a place.'

The living room is where Romi unwinds in the evening. She enjoys lighting scented candles and a fire in winter. 'I also love relaxing in my bedroom – it's one of my favourite rooms in the house,' she says. 'I have a gorgeous little balcony off it with beautiful cacti, and from my bed I can look out through the shutters to my bougainvillea and palm trees. I could be anywhere in the world. I absolutely adore it.'

Romi Weinberg

When I do less…
it recharges me. I thrive on being busy with projects that interest me, but I also enjoy having downtime to reconnect and clear my mind. There needs to be a balance.

When I disconnect…
I can give my undivided attention to the people who matter most in my life. I have a rule that we're not allowed to use our phones during mealtimes and that's really important to me. When we're all at the table, we need to be present and have meaningful conversations and listen to each other.

I have learnt to live without…
a partner. I'm so proud of myself to not rely on anyone else, and parent on my own.

I set boundaries around…
how people can affect my emotions. I don't let other people's views or actions change or bother me. This is something that has definitely come with age.

Calm is…
when things make sense in my mind.

Change is…
wonderful. I thrive off it.

When it comes to order and chaos in my life…
I can move from one to the other quite easily. My life is orderly because I am a very organised, neat person, and I like to know where I'm going and have a plan. But, at the same time, I absolutely love spontaneity and doing things on a whim. I embrace unplanned moments and events.

I care less about…
sweating the small stuff. I used to do it a lot, but then life events put into perspective what's really important. I try not to focus on things that aren't part of the big picture.

I care more about…
being the best version of me – an amazing mum to my children, a beautiful sister, a loving daughter and a caring friend. Having creativity in my life is also really important.

My life feels meaningful when…
my children have learnt something from me. I love nothing more than realising I've taught my daughters even the smallest things. To me, that is everything.

What's most important in my life right now is…
that my daughters are happy and safe, that I am bringing them up as strong, resilient, kind women.

**EMBRACING SLOW –
SUSTAINABLE, LOCAL, ORGANIC, WHOLE:**

Sustainable living means…
embracing pre-loved wares. I love vintage pieces and objects that have a story and a history. I know that I'll always love pieces that are not trend-driven. I have many antiques and vintage wares in my home, which I adore. They give it character and charm.

Local is…
part of my everyday life. I buy pretty much everything from my local shops – from the butcher, the fish shop and grocery store. We all know each other by name and I've built great relationships with all of them over the past decade of living in this area.

Organic is…
everything to me in terms of design. I love things that are imperfect. I love organic, raw, natural states.

I feel Whole when…
my children are with me.

ELISE PIOCH CHAPPELL & PAUL CHAPPELL

Béziers, France

'I love life next to my family. You need less here – less money and there is less pressure – because you're in the countryside. And just when you think you've arrived in the smallest, most traditional sleepy village, you realise that other people like us have fallen for the charm of the Tuesday morning market. And I say, do we realise how lucky we are to live in this slow community?'

A few years ago, Elise Pioch Chappell was talking to a friend about her grandparents, describing her childhood in the South of France, when she realised she wanted her daughter, Loulou, to have similar adventures. 'I had such a happy childhood – one surrounded by nature – and I wanted to share some of what I had with her, at least a taste of it,' she says. 'I was crying about my grandparents and understood I was missing my family too much. From that came the seed of an idea that I was too far from them.'

At the time Elise was living in Sydney with her husband, Paul 'Pablo' Chappell, and Loulou, who is now six. They were dividing their time between an apartment at the back of the warehouse for her homewares business, Maison Balzac, in Botany and a converted nineteenth-century church on the Hawkesbury River. For the next year, Elise spent many evenings searching online for properties in and around Béziers, where her parents still live in her childhood home. One night she found a place that met all of her criteria: it was near her parents' place, it was in a village, had a garden, the house had retained all of its original features – and the price was right. Elise called her parents and asked them to look at it for her.

'Because they know me so well, they said it was exactly what I was looking for – although it hadn't been looked after for a good fifteen years,' she says. Two weeks later, Elise arrived on Bastille Day to view the home. 'As I walked in and saw the corridor and tiles, I thought, done, this is it,' she says. 'I called Pabs and said, "I think we've got our house. This is our new life."'

The house, a nineteenth-century *maison de maître*, originally belonged to vineyard owners. It had been decorated only twice. The first time was in the 1880s when it was built, and included features such as patterned tiles, ornate mouldings and wall frescoes. The second owner, the village doctor, bought the house in the 1960s and restored it with his wife. 'Now it's having a third touch – our touch,' Elise says.

The doctor and his wife lived in the house until their deaths at 103 and 102, respectively. 'Maybe this house is the secret to a long life,' Elise says. 'It has a garden and lots of space, and was filled with literature and art. I think they had a beautiful life here. Homes can give you that energy. If you are happy in your home, I think your life unfolds from there.'

Elise never returned to Sydney, and Pablo and Loulou soon joined her, but not in their new home; instead they had to live for a while at her parents' place. It took them eight months of legal wrangling to free the house from the estate. 'I managed to reunite three members of the family who hadn't spoken to each other for twenty years,' Elise says. Finally, on Valentine's Day 2018, with the house covered in snow, Elise and Pablo got the keys.

They had only one suitcase each, having sold their church on the Hawkesbury River furnished. However, their new home was still filled with the doctor's furniture and possessions. 'When we bought it you couldn't see the walls, they were covered with cabinets,' Elise says. 'What was in the house was more expensive than the actual house. The government spent two days assigning value to all the goods, and what the family didn't want we could buy. They were emptying it for days and days and days. At one stage the process became overwhelming. But I got back three days later and discovered my house.'

Even though vast quantities of furniture and items were removed, a lot remained. The kitchen had everything in it – from a bottle opener to a colander – it all just needed a thorough clean. 'This is something we massively believe in,' Elise says. 'We feel there is so much quality stuff in the world that we shouldn't be buying new stuff.' And when they do need something, they go to a local flea market. 'We love the idea that it's one less piece that's going in the garbage, and it's one more piece that is going to be used and recycled.'

Pablo says that they take this approach with everything. They have bought a second-hand washing machine and other appliances. 'There are a lot of things that were built in the 1990s that just don't break,' he says. 'The car we drive is twenty years old, but it is so well built that it keeps on going. I feel the best thing you can do for the planet is to buy good-quality second-hand.'

The couple feel just as passionate about respecting the history of the home. 'Many people don't know what to do with these houses,' Elise says. 'We wanted just to run with it and add our own touches, but really try to respect it. Because we love it. Today it would be hard to reproduce these kinds of details. And you realise the quality of the materials – the ceilings, everything. It would cost a fortune.' Plus, they don't want to rush into decoration. 'Our previous home took ten years to restore,' Elise says. 'We always take it super slow.'

They have made some changes, though. An island bench was added to the kitchen and a bath to Loulou's ensuite. They removed the wallpaper in some areas. 'It's like reading the story of the house and peeling the layers,' Elise says. However, they engaged artists to restore the murals in the upstairs and downstairs hallways.

It hasn't always been easy to stick to their vision of celebrating the original features of the home. Along the way many locals have offered lots of advice on how they should modernise the building. One person recommended they lower the ceilings and use polystyrene to insulate the walls and hide electrical wires, to keep the rooms warmer in winter. Someone else said to replace the original windows with PVC. They were also told that Pablo's idea for a granite kitchen island bench wasn't possible. 'Whatever you do that's new you will always find people who say you can't do that,' Elise says. It's a lesson that Pablo learnt early in his career as an industrial designer at Dyson: when you hit a hurdle, try again. Having no luck in getting the benchtop made locally, they found someone in Spain who brought their idea to life.

But despite a few setbacks, Elise and Pablo love village life. 'It's real France,' he says. 'It's not touched by tourism or Disneyland like Provence.' Their favourite day is Tuesday when they go to the local market and buy fresh produce that's in season. 'You have no packaging and no plastic – it's from your hand to your basket,' Elise says. 'When I shut my computer I have that life on my doorstep. I love that balance. I am very lucky.'

Elise Pioch Chappell & Paul Chappell

COPENHAGEN JAZZ FESTIVAL · 40TH EDITION · JULY 6-15, 2018

Elise Pioch Chappell & Paul Chappell

When I do less…
I feel lighter. The more I do, the heavier and slower I seem to get. The less I do, the more I feel free and light, and I can go forward.

When I disconnect…
it's always related to food. I'm either shopping for food or cooking. I think of the pleasure that I'm going to give people when I make food for them.

I have learnt to live without…
things. The more we get rid of things and the less we buy, the happier we get.

I set boundaries around…
meals. Breakfast, lunch and dinner are for sitting around the table together having a homemade meal. When we are home, that's what we do. That's how I was raised and I think it's a beautiful ritual to keep going.

Calm is…
my home. To me it's calming because it's to my taste, so I really love being surrounded by what I've created; it feels balanced. When I'm surrounded by beauty it recharges the batteries and I feel my best.

Change is…
constant. Inevitable and energising and exhausting.

When it comes to order and chaos in my life…
we need both. I'm such an ordered person. When it's messy it impacts my soul so much that I'm not happy and I can't work. I don't think it's a good thing because I rely too much on order. My way to fight it is to provoke the chaos. When things are too ordered and routine I have to come back in and do something. I need both – I couldn't just be in chaos and couldn't just be in an ordered life.

I care less about…
expectations that I set myself. But when they pushed me to the edge I realised I had made up those expectations and so, in the same way that I created them, I could lower them. Now I'm starting to care less about expectations. I'm not there yet but I'm learning and it's working.

I care more about…
my own family, Pablo and Loulou. That and my mental health and wellbeing. In the list of priorities, it was always Loulou and Pablo and then myself. And now I'm learning to be higher up on the list of nurturing myself. Again, I'm not there yet but little things are helping.

My life feels meaningful when…
I'm in the moment. I have a tendency to look forward to things or look back to things, but I think it's so much more meaningful to be there right in the moment. It's also part of a process.

What's most important in my life right now is…
to find the one place that would be the anchor for the rest of our lives.

**EMBRACING SLOW –
SUSTAINABLE, LOCAL, ORGANIC, WHOLE:**

Sustainable living means…
using second-hand everything: homes, cars, furniture, clothes. To me, that is sustainable to the max. And there is so much joy in the process of finding.

Local is…
being connected to our natural surrounds. Once a week we go foraging and find fruits, herbs and wild asparagus – that knowledge of what surrounds you, what is wild and what nature gives you, doesn't cost anything. I think it has set me apart all of my life to have that knowledge. When I was a child, I would go fishing, hunting or foraging for food with my parents. Even when I was working in fashion, to have that knowledge has always grounded me. To be humble and have humility has been super important to me, as well as to know you can survive in the wild. I know too many people who won't eat an oyster from a rock

because they don't know what shop it's from. When we go to the beach with Loulou, we go through the sand dunes and if we find a weed called *salicorne* we pick and eat it. I'm so happy she knows that. In Australia it took me a few years to find my habits. When we got back here it was amazing to show Loulou what I've learnt and all the plants and herbs I know so well. That awareness of your surroundings is so important and grounding.

Organic is…
what you grow yourself. In our garden we have wild asparagus, verbena, two types of figs and six mulberry trees. We never treat anything with chemicals. Organic is when you have full visibility or control of how something is grown.

That's something I've learnt from my family circle. My older brother is a marine biologist, which came from a passion for scuba diving, and we only eat the fish that he catches. He catches in the wild. He never kills the females or fish that are endangered. We can't ask everyone to have that knowledge, but it is something that I respect. In the wintertime, my dad hunts birds that are listed as pests. On the weekend we go to his house and eat food we have plucked. We respect the lives of the animals and never kill more than we eat, and that's how I see organic.

I feel Whole when…
I am with my family and surrounded by nature.

MERCEDES LOPEZ COELLO

Moscari, Mallorca, Spain

'This home is a sanctuary where we come and connect, and not just with ourselves but with our family. It is the base for everything.'

When Mercedes Lopez Coello was living in Sweden, she would often dream of having a home in Tuscany. Her husband Mads said, 'That's because you haven't been to Mallorca.' At the time, Mercedes considered the Balearic island to be mainly a charter holiday destination. However, Mads had seen a different side to Mallorca, having spent time there while working in film post production, and he encouraged Mercedes to experience the 'real' Mallorca. When she did, her response was immediate. 'I was just in love,' she says. Four months later, the couple packed two suitcases and a dog and moved to the island permanently.

'It was a fresh start to come here and rediscover myself,' Mercedes says. Initially the couple rented a house in Sineu, about half an hour from the capital city, Palma. 'We had to drive up a hill, and the road was bad. That was a good sign: secluded on a hill,' Mercedes says. They lived there for five years before buying a stone house in Llubí, where their sons Oliver, now twelve, and Felix, nine, were born. However, once the boys started school the family moved to Palma and remain based there. Oliver and Felix can walk to school through the woods, and now they're both older, they enjoy being connected to friends. But since buying a country hideaway in Moscari, Mercedes sometimes finds herself asking why she doesn't spend more time there. 'It is really something else,' she says.

The decision to buy a place in the hills came about five years ago, and their stone *finca* – farmhouse – was one of the first places they saw. The agent didn't have the key so they were only able to view the house from the outside, but they didn't mind because they had only intended to get a general feeling for the house and location. 'We just looked at each other. That was enough. We loved the area and the energy,' Mercedes says. 'We have lots of good memories of living in Llubí, and for me Moscari was a lot like that first love with Mallorca,' Mercedes says. 'We wanted that same feeling.'

When Mercedes first arrived in Mallorca, she couldn't understand why many chose to have a second home on the island, often only thirty minutes away. But after moving to Palma, she has a new perspective. 'Palma can be a stressful city,' she says. 'In the summer you don't want to be there – that's when all the tourists come, and it's so hot. In the country you have the breeze and you can see the stars. You come to these villages and it's so peaceful.' And while Mercedes enjoys the cafes, restaurants and cultural events in Palma during other times of the year, life in the country offers something else. 'This is the Mallorca that I knew eighteen years ago,' she says. 'The younger helping the elderly, people in cafes having a morning coffee, the old men with their hats driving mopeds. There is still a sense of community here.'

The house in Moscari previously belonged to an older German couple. They had maintained the 100-year-old building well. 'When we arrived here I felt the energy of the place was very soothing, and there was a lot of harmony in the area. Not just in the house but all around it,' Mercedes says. However, the kitchen was quite small and closed off, in part because of a guest toilet on the ground floor. At first Mercedes was only going to make a few changes. 'And then you start hammering and find areas that need fixing, and you think that because we've done that, we might as well finish off another area,' she says. The biggest change was to tear down one of the bathrooms, remove the guest toilet and enlarge the kitchen area.

The project was Mercedes' first renovation. 'I had no idea where to start,' she says. 'But in the back of my mind I was very clear – I wanted to be very austere and use a lot of natural materials: wood, stone, ceramics, linen, rattan. And I wanted everything to feel that it was made by hand. Nothing is straight – a lot of these details were in the house originally. Anything that was new followed the style of the imperfections. Instead of using straight corners for the edges, they feel organic and blend in.' The furniture and decor are a collection of pieces that Mercedes has slowly accumulated over the years – from her time living in Sweden, as well as during her travels.

When it came to the exterior of the building, she didn't want to make any major changes. 'For me, it was super clear not to touch the outside,' Mercedes says. She freshened the paint on the timber shutters using the same colour as they had been previously, and they restored some of the stonework, but were careful to choose the right colour so the exterior appeared unchanged. 'I wanted any changes to blend in and make it appear as if it had always been there,' she says. The garden remained largely untouched, too. Anything that she has planted – lavender, sage, rosemary – blends in with the existing foliage and plants. 'My garden is not polished,' she says. 'I like it natural, so I try not to interfere too much.' The result is a place where Mercedes feels that she can

relax. 'It's so soothing,' she says. 'The house says, "come, embrace".' Living modestly also has benefits. 'It's small, so when we spend time together here we become closer,' Mercedes says. 'I miss having that togetherness when we're not here.'

The house in Moscari is where Mercedes is able to reconnect with nature and herself. 'When I come here, I lay in the hammock for ten minutes and then there is a soft breeze and a sunbeam of light and butterflies,' she says. 'You realise you can let go.'

Mercedes Lopez Coello

Mercedes Lopez Coello

When I do less…
I feel at ease. But I can also feel guilty and
relieved. It's a process whereby I have to let go.
I have to say to myself, no 'musts', and just be
in the moment instead of thinking of all the
things I have to do.

When I disconnect…
I feel in balance – that everything is as it should
be. It's very comforting when you really feel it
inside your body and in your core, as opposed
to just saying it.

I have learnt to live without…
complications. I have learnt to live simply.
That's my motto now – to try to keep things
simple. This house symbolically has shown
me that we don't need a lot. It's so uncluttered
and my eyes can rest easily. It's a completely
different style of house to the one we have
in Palma, which is also harmonious and
a sanctuary, but it's much more bohemian
and chaotic. I like to come here and enjoy
the simplicity of this place.

I set boundaries around…
anything that takes my energy negatively
and that I feel affects me in a physical way.
I've always been a giver, but am more aware
that it can be better to help someone to
help themselves.

Calm is…
a moment to myself in nature.

Change is…
growth. To change something you transform
it so it grows. And as it grows it transforms.

When it comes to order and chaos
in my life…
I have it fifty-fifty. But I am working on having
more order in my life, and that's why this house
is somewhere I enjoy being.

I care less about…
expectations. I guess it comes with age.
It's so relieving. Just to say this is who
I am and feel good about it.

I care more about…
the environment.

My life feels meaningful when…
my family are in harmony and happy. Then it
feels as if I've succeeded. My success relates
a lot to my family life. I am aware that my
values live on through my sons, and while they
are individuals they are also part of my legacy.

What's most important in my life
right now is…
my family. I always go back to my family.

**EMBRACING SLOW –
SUSTAINABLE, LOCAL, ORGANIC, WHOLE:**

Sustainable living means…
living in the rhythm of nature. Often we need
to slow the pace of life and keep it simple.

Local is…
important in so many areas of our lives: local
food and production, as well as living in sync
with the seasons. I have my own veggie garden,
which helps me stay in tune with nature. And
when building this house, I used many local
artisans and handcrafts.

Organic is…
again, being in tune with nature. For me, it's
not natural to use pesticides on food. I think
nature is so wise and has all the information
that it needs. It doesn't need humans to
interfere and manipulate it. It has ancient
knowledge that's already all there.

I feel Whole when…
I'm in nature. That's why I love this place.
When I eat healthily, sleep well and exercise –
and do the things I love from the heart –
that's when I'm balanced.

'Don't
explain your
philosophy.
Embody it.'

Epictetus

SLOW

How can we take a more thoughtful approach to the way we live at home? While we may want to make better choices, the process can sometimes feel like another 'to-do' to add to the list. And that is not the idea behind slow living. The first step is both the simplest and the hardest. We need to build a pause into our decision-making and be more considered with what we consume – from goods, media, marketing and messages, to unwanted advice and opinions, which sometimes are our own. It is a skill that benefits not just the environment and our bank balance but also our sense of wellbeing.

When we learn how to be still and live in the moment we have greater clarity about what's most important within our home life. What are we doing right now? It can be a task – because there are always many of those. Even something as simple as doing the laundry can bring pleasure when we pay attention to the sun shining on our face, are awake to birdsong, smell the flowers in bloom, and feel the warm fabric between our fingers. When we are present we can feel more grateful for all that we have. When we focus on the real beauty of our life – and not what we think will buy us happiness – there is less room for dissatisfaction, comparison and greed. It awakens kindness for ourselves and our journey.

There are many ways to embrace SLOW choices – Sustainable, Local, Organic, Whole – at home. We can create a space that meets our needs, but it doesn't have to meet all of our desires at once. We can look to salvage yards, street finds, vintage and second-hand wares before buying new. We can take our time and renovate slowly, perhaps one room at a time. Or prioritise different areas of our home in different seasons. Because sometimes we have to ease off certain projects so others can flourish. Similar to playing a piece of music, our homes can work well when there are different tempos at varying times. There is no right and wrong. And while we can learn from other people's experiences, we have to trust our own judgements because we live with our decisions. We can find a good balance – one that suits our lives – and find more pleasure in the process.

The slow movement has evolved and grown significantly since its early days in Italy more than thirty years ago. However, the core ideas remain the same. On the following pages are the central tenets that are still relevant today, providing guidelines on how we can become more conscious about the way we live our lives. Let's also take a moment to consider that how we live at home has ramifications the world over. To paraphrase zero-waste chef Anne-Marie Bonneau: *The world doesn't need a handful of people embracing SLOW living perfectly, but millions living these ideas imperfectly.* And if we each take responsibility for how we live, we can enjoy the benefits together.

SUSTAINABLE

While we might want to be more informed citizens, and create more sustainable homes, what does that actually mean? We are exposed to an overwhelming amount of information, and misinformation, when it comes to building and furnishing sustainably. By definition, 'sustainable' is something that can be maintained at a certain rate. But to live in this way there needs to be more education. Rarely is the supply chain of manufacturing transparent, and we don't always know the materials and conditions of production. For example, the words 'natural' and 'sustainable' are often used interchangeably, but that can be misleading. All woods are natural, but not all of them are sustainable. While bamboo is fast growing and can be harvested within a few years, some species of mahogany and teak are depleted. Organisations such as the Forest Stewardship Council help to provide consumers with clear guidelines on which timbers have been derived from responsibly managed forests. Educating ourselves on the materials we use – where they're from, as well as their environmental credentials – is key. But sometimes it's simpler to re-use what we've already got.

We can also create more sustainable homes when we design them for the climate, not against it. Orientating the main living areas for passive shading in the summer and good solar capture during winter can help to reduce our energy usage, as well as enhance our experience of the home. We can also insulate walls, the ceiling and underfloor for more efficient heating and to save on energy costs; utilise double-glazed windows or curtains with thermal backing; and install water- and energy-saving devices and a rainwater collection tank. Even planting gardens with native and local plants or drought-tolerant species can have a positive impact. But we can get more creative too and consider waste-free living, permaculture or some form of self-sufficiency. However, if we feel overwhelmed by all the options and decisions, it's good to remember that the most important step is the first one. And when we talk about our choices, we start to normalise them too. Conservation and conversation go hand-in-hand. Greater awareness over the proliferation of single-use plastic, for example, has started to change our perceptions and consumption. Change is possible. And coming.

LOCAL

While we often think about 'local' in terms of proximity to where we live, it is a way of living that can combat globalisation. Carbon emissions are the greatest threat to the environment, but less are produced when we shop and support local businesses and industry. Buying local also means less packaging is required. We can pick produce straight from a farmer's market stand into a basket and carry it into our kitchen. We can buy a dining table from a local maker using FSC timber without the need for shipping containers. And when we connect with makers we can develop an appreciation for the value of the product too. We can request custom details or modifications to tailor it to our needs, and learn how to care for the materials so they last longer. And when we appreciate the value of the product, we are more likely to get it fixed or repaired. It may also be something we want to hold on to longer and pass down from one generation to the next.

Human connection is one of the most important elements of a meaningful life. It is why we get pleasure from having coffee in a cafe or buying wares directly from a maker. The etymology of the word community can be traced back to the Latin *communitas* – *cum* (with/together) and *munus* (gift). When we connect with people and have a shared sense of responsibility and common goals, we can thrive together. Engaging with our local community comes with many benefits – and not just produce swaps. When we connect and are on good terms with our neighbours, there are more safe places for our children to play, or we can carpool. We can also share knowledge and ideas, laugh and feel valued. A sense of community can also contribute to social capital – the networks that help a society function effectively.

Social engagement can even help to extend our lifespan, especially when we surround ourselves with those who share the same values and healthy lifestyle. It is one of nine defining characteristics of people who live in Blue Zones – geographic regions of the world that are home to some of the world's oldest people. Other features include regular low-intensity physical activity, moderate caloric intake, a plant-based diet, red wine in moderation, a sense of life purpose, slowing down to relieve stress, spiritual or religious engagement, and prioritising family. Author Dan Buettner says slowing down is a thread that runs through the various ways people live in all of these areas. It is a way of living that can add a richness of experience to our daily lives.

Connecting to our local environment is equally important. We enhance our experience of it when we get out and about. Engaging with others in our local area is also important. This can be anything from walking along a high street or nature trail to attending a local market or fair. We are more likely to make the environment a priority when it is a part of our life. And as we know, spending time outdoors is also good for our physical and mental health, and can help to reduce stress levels. For children, it can encourage exercise, increase self-esteem, teach them how to take risks and foster their creativity. Our natural environment isn't just something to behold, though. We can integrate it into our lives through the way we build and design our homes. Even the simple gesture of using branches as decoration or displaying local seed pods can help us to feel more connected. Because while we can read about its benefits, we all know how much better we feel after spending time outdoors and engaging with our local environment.

ORGANIC

While we may often consider organic in relation to the food we eat, we can also take it to mean non-mass-produced. Small-scale production has tangible benefits for local communities and for the creation of our homes. Supporting local trades and producers helps to sustain local employment too.

Organic can also mean that a product or material is free of chemicals. This is becoming increasingly important as we consider the impact of chemicals on our health and environment. While the first artificial fertilisers were created in the mid-nineteenth century, it wasn't until the 1940s that chemical pesticides became popularised. In some ways the term 'organic' is a misnomer because it describes food and materials in their natural state. Everything else is non-organic, processed or synthetic. When it comes to our homes, there are also many objects that are made and finished with chemicals, some of which can be harmful to our health and the environment – volatile organic compounds in paints and sealants, and formaldehyde in mattresses, for example – and that is to say nothing of all the chemicals in many household cleaning and personal care products. We can go a step further and question the impact that living near phone towers – and sleeping beside technology devices – has on our health. Not everything that we consume is visible or tangible.

Building biology is a growing area of interest for proponents of natural living, and raises important questions. We spend a lot of time and money in and on our homes; however, we are mostly unaware of the chemicals that surround us on a daily basis and the impact that they have on our health. There are more than 113 million chemicals registered for use on the world's largest chemical database, but how many can we actually name and what do we know about them? Yet we live alongside them and consume great quantities every day. Some lessons have been learnt too late when it comes to the use of asbestos, leaded paint and other chemicals such as benzene and vinyl chloride, which is used to make PVC for pipes, wires and cable coatings and is a known carcinogen. The statistics are sobering, and should make us stop for a moment to consider the materials and products that we allow into our homes.

WHOLE

We can embrace slow living at home when we take a more whole-istic approach to our decisions. Holism – or wholism – is based upon the idea that we should view systems as wholes, not just a collection of parts. When we live on a rural property with a well or septic tank, we might consider the impact of chemicals from cleaning and personal care products on our water supply. As with Newton's third law of motion in physics – for every action there is an equal and opposite reaction – our choices have an impact on other areas of our life, and the world. Similarly, when we buy soap in plastic bottles, no matter how aesthetically pleasing, we should acknowledge that there is a ripple effect – from the resources required to create and ship the bottle, to recycling it. It's time to build a pause in our lives before we consume.

Let's end our perceived culture of convenience. And focus on the values we want to live by. What will be our legacy? Within our homes we are ideally placed to make real and meaningful change. Let's find a moment of still to embrace the principles of slow living at home. Let's begin today.

EMMA & TOM LANE

Byron Bay, New South Wales, Australia

'In a world where there is so much doing and moving from thought to thought and from one action to another, we have forgotten how to be still, to stop and be a human BE-ing – just being still and enjoying this moment in time.'

In a short time, Emma and Tom Lane have become well known in the Northern New South Wales region of Australia, in large part due to their project, The Farm, at Byron Bay, a collective of micro-businesses that operate under the overarching principle of 'Grow, Feed, Educate'. However, it is on their property in the hinterland, The Range, that they are engaged in a more personal project – reconsidering the idea of how to create a home.

It took the couple ten years to find a place to bring their vision to life. At the start of the journey they were living in Sydney but also owned a holiday house in the hinterland town of Federal. 'It was a wonderful balance to live in the city and then spend holidays in the hills, surrounded by nature,' Emma says.

However, four years ago they decided to make the move a permanent one. 'We moved for the closeness to nature, the slower pace and to create a legacy project, The Farm at Byron Bay,' Emma says. 'We feel more connected to community here, surrounded by creative and dynamic people all trying to make a difference. I love that the majority of people have moved here for the same reasons.'

After moving to the area, Emma and Tom soon realised they wanted to live on a property with a minimum of 100 acres, but also one that was only a five minutes' drive to a village such as Bangalow or Newrybar. A distant ocean view would be a bonus, too. Ten years after they began their initial search, their patience paid off. The Range is on top of a ridgeline that is one of the highest points in the Byron hinterland, and offers them everything on their wishlist. 'This is somewhere we can watch the world roll by and see our children running around and enjoying nature, and having a taste of the childhood that we had,' Emma says. 'We have found home.'

The process of creating this dream life has taken time for them to realise, too. The couple bought the property in July 2017 and over the next eighteen months lived in town during the week and spent their weekends in a small cabin on the land while building and making adjustments to the homestead in which they now live.

The existing house, built in the 1980s, didn't have as strong a sense of connection to the land as Emma and Tom had envisaged for their new home. While they kept the original slab, some walls and part of the roof, they changed the aesthetics. 'We wanted to add layers of texture and create a feeling of history, as if the house had been here a long time,' Emma says. 'Although it was forty years old, we wanted it to have more stories to tell, which is why we layered in many old and recycled elements.'

For the meantime, they have kept the main homestead to only three bedrooms. Brothers Charlie, fourteen, and George, eleven, share a room, as do sisters Matilda, nine, and Lulu, seven. The house is smaller than the previous ones they have owned and built, and while there are plans to eventually add more bedrooms in the courtyard area at the back of the house, the couple's focus was to keep everyone physically close. 'We are only building what we need now, and with 120 acres to play with, we can always expand later,' Emma says. 'Keeping the house to a smaller scale also meant we had more budget to finish it to a higher specification and make it as beautiful as we could, rather than spreading the budget across a larger construction. Plus, you never know what might change in the future – the kids may never want their own room!'

The couple have a master plan for the entire property, but each section is designed in its own right, so they can be flexible about when they activate a particular part of the building process. 'Ultimately, the land around the house is the playground and the home is the heart,' Emma says.

Connecting to the land and the region has played a big role in the creation of the homestead. They have been conscious of using local tradesmen and artisans who have, in turn, used resources as local to the area as possible. And they have encouraged their children to help with regeneration planting, building stone paths and collecting firewood from old fallen trees in the forests. 'Getting the whole family involved and having fun while doing chores can help reframe what sometimes can be a little mundane but essential in everyday home life,' Emma says. 'Having a conscience for the environment is also an important value for our family. Like a lot of things, this is a great way to start educating kids at home in a subtle and positive way.'

Q

When I do less…
I feel more connected to life and the greater, larger, more expansive world out there.

When I disconnect…
my world seems to flow better, and the creative opportunities open up.

I have learnt to live without…
a lot of clutter.

I set boundaries around…
who I spend time with and what I give to others.

Calm is…
being unflappable and centred, when my heart rate is in rhythm with nature.

Change is…
necessary for the evolution of self, but should not be used to avoid uncomfortable moments, as it's in discomfort that we grow.

When it comes to order and chaos in my life…
I prefer order, which in turn gives me more freedom in many other aspects, but if life becomes too ordered I choose a little chaos to shake it up. Ultimately, the balance of both is a perfect way to exist.

I care less about…
what people think. Finally!

I care more about…
the environment and future for my children.

My life feels meaningful when…
I am living in the now and surrounded by people I love and who value me.

What's most important in my life right now is…
being mindful and conscious, being present with my family, and creating projects with substance and meaning that leave a legacy.

A

EMBRACING SLOW –
SUSTAINABLE, LOCAL, ORGANIC, WHOLE:

Sustainable living means…
making decisions now that make the future life on this planet viable.

Local is…
looking after those in your community.

Organic is…
as close to nature as possible.

I feel Whole when…
I'm living with purpose and doing instinctively what is right.

THE REIMAGINED HOME

What are the key questions we should ask before building or changing our homes?
It is often all too easy to default to established ideas and methods without considering
if they are the best solution for the site and a sustainable future. Emma Lane, co-founder
of The Farm Byron Bay, recommends that perhaps instead we should consider the
land, the materials available and how our home needs to function.

Emma Lane

Last year our family travelled to Japan for the first time, and it was a cultural and sensory adventure on so many levels. We landed in Tokyo and as we drove into the city, I was struck by how new, shiny and modern all the buildings were. One of the great joys of travelling is finding that beautiful balance of both old and new reflected in the buildings and landscape. It was in my naivety, and then my subsequent questioning to the locals, that the reality of the situation dawned on me. One elderly gentleman explained that there was no 'real old' left in Tokyo because the city had been flattened during the war seventy-five years ago. He told us that we would need to go to Kyoto to discover the culture and the original buildings that we were seeking.

There was great sadness in this story on many levels, but what particularly struck me was the loss of that history, and the story that is felt and told in the bones of an old house or place. When considering the options of what to do with our land and the old homestead at The Range, this was really important to us. The original house on the property had elements that we liked, but these weren't necessarily what we had in mind for the way we wanted to live and our vision for the next chapter on this land. What I find magical in homes with character and warmth are the layers of stories from different periods. We can still pay respect to the past without limiting our plans for what may unfold in the build.

In the early days of The Range's formation, we immersed ourselves in design, creating several plans for the homestead that involved building from scratch, until we caught ourselves and changed our thinking more towards using elements from the existing architecture. This enquiry uncovered how we could work with what was currently here while embracing part of the site's heritage and actual elements of the land. The stumbling block for me when thinking about demolishing the house was how we would deal with the old concrete slab from the house. We would simply have to bury it somewhere on our land and this didn't seem right when we could potentially incorporate it in our new design. It was then that we made the decision not to demolish, a choice that would not necessarily save us money but would indirectly and subtly treat the planet with more kindness. We would work with what we had, merge old with new to savour the history and keep some chapters of that earlier story alive.

This change in mindset set us off on a delightful journey, and we found ourselves taking this evolutionary thinking far more seriously, incorporating the re-use, repurpose and upcycle model where we could. This was wonderfully liberating after a period of living in a way that was a little less considered, and in a society with a preference for a more disposable way of existing. Our resources on this planet are not guaranteed to last forever, and the statistics showing the volume of material going to landfill is quite frightening.

Consideration of the land when building is paramount. It is the earth, along with clever engineering, that holds our structures up and together they provide the foundation for our homes. With this in mind, we set about finding a geomancist – a land healer – to help us determine if our 120 acres were in good order energetically, and to check the earth for geopathic stress. This can be powerful in balancing the earth's energy. This process has now created a parcel of land that not only looks in keeping with its environment but also feels balanced and peaceful.

Before we began planning the structure of the building, we considered the land and what materials it could naturally provide us in order to prevent resource wastage. With the help of a talented local stonemason, we uncovered basalt rocks that had been on this farmland for thousands of years, and had been moved to the remnant rainforests when the land had previously been cleared. We used these existing rocks in the construction of our retaining walls and fireplaces. For the assembly of the walls, our stonemason trained in the old way of building rock walls, building a wall that allowed us to be authentic to the old ways of building and also to the land. The finished stone wall sits comfortably into the landscape and house design. We wanted our home to blend into the ridgeline when viewed from a distance, and to look like it corresponded to the landscape – these stone walls help achieve this.

In stonework, we also created a large amphitheatre-style fire pit, as Tom loves slow-cooking over an open fire. This area was where the old water tank used to sit, and leaving it empty serves as a reminder of what used to be there. As the geomancist explained to us, the land too has scars and fractures, so rather than creating new ones by excavating or filling the space, it was literally reimagined into another use. The repurposed space now provides a connection both to its past and to its continuing story.

Timber, although a renewable resource, lends itself well to recycling and upcycling. We took many of the old timber bones from the original house into the new homestead. Doorframes found a new life as timber shelves, and large recycled timber beams were used to hold up our roof. A large piece of hoop pine from the surf club in Byron Bay is now our family dining table, and two large five-metre slabs of 200-year-old Australian teak were repurposed as a large outdoor dining table.

Our floor tiles are recycled terracotta roof tiles from a demolished *casa* in Croatia. I wanted to find a floor surface that would blend into the earth's rich colour so that we didn't need to be precious about dirt and mud trails on the floor – especially when living with four active children and a dog. For decking we used old sleepers, which are both robust and hardwearing. Equally, the corten cabinetry in the kitchen blends into the earthy tones and is highly practical. This is where considering the function of how you want to live is important when choosing materials for your home – it can make living and enjoying your space effortless and more relevant.

There are many benefits that come from creating a well-crafted home. We were able to engage old trades and artisans, who are employed less and less these days, as they are seemingly expensive when compared with the use of machinery- and factory-built items. But the question I ask myself is what character and energy would I prefer my home to possess and be imagined from? The personality and essence of something hand-built that has taken the commitment of time and been touched by human hands or the detached attributes of a rapidly made factory product? The slow pace of humanity or the frantic energy of fast-paced machinery? I know what I prefer.

As we learnt in Tokyo, it's not always possible to keep our history alive, but we do have a choice to layer our homes with stories of the past. Knowing we have created a home with substance, with a consciousness for sustainability, and honouring the traditional slow techniques of the past is a step in the right direction towards living more in harmony with our surrounds. This all leads to an exciting and optimistic new attitude to building and construction.

EMMA LANE is co-founder of The Farm Byron Bay, a collective of micro-businesses on an eighty-acre farm that is focused on a mission to 'Grow, Feed, Educate'. The mother of four is also co-author of a book about that project, *The Farm Community*. Continuing her advocacy for conservation and community, Emma has co-created The Beach House East Coast, an environmentally conscious private hire venue.

Emma Lane

JULI DAOUST BAKER & JOHN BAKER

Stirling, Ontario, Canada

'This home feels happy and solid, which creates a sense of security that allows us to give ourselves over to just being.'

For ten years, Juli Daoust Baker and John Baker have been living in Toronto in a home above their design shop, Mjölk. However, a couple of years after the birth of their youngest child, Howell, now five, who is brother to Elodie, seven, they started to consider the idea of finding a home that wasn't so entwined with work – a place in the country where they could retreat on weekends and summer break. Both Juli and John grew up visiting their respective grandparents on farms and were keen for their children to have some of that experience. 'We are not pioneers or trying to romanticise that type of life,' John says. 'But we had those Huck Finn experiences as kids, and we were nostalgic for our children to have similar adventures too.'

Once the seed had been planted, John became interested in stone houses, feeling a connection to them because of his Scottish ancestry. Not long afterwards, in August 2016, the couple made their way a couple of hours east of Toronto to rural Ontario. 'The city comes with you in some places,' John says. 'But it's a different culture here – there are not a lot of Torontonians.' What they found was a building that dates to about 1840 with only two previous owners, the most recent living until he was over 100 years old. The house was not in a good condition. It didn't have any integrated plumbing or electricity, the main living area had been abandoned for at least ten years, and the rest of the house seemed as if it hadn't been touched for many years. 'The previous owner kept adding layers of linoleum to waterproof the floors, and drop ceilings were made of Styrofoam,' John says. 'Everything was just floating. It felt as if you could push a wall down.'

The couple immediately signed papers to purchase the two-acre property; however, they had to wait for a year for severance from a larger 600-acre parcel of agricultural land to come through. 'Despite its dilapidated condition, the house had a solidity that was very reassuring,' Juli says. It had been built from stones unearthed from when the surrounding fields were originally ploughed.

When they first saw the house they were attracted to its location, nestled within rolling hills and enveloped on three sides by fields of corn.

'We were looking for a place where we could engage with nature. There was a peaceful magic about the property,' Juli says. 'We were also very excited to have so much variety of space to explore – a stream, an orchard, an open field, and two copses of trees for imaginative play for our children.' Their nearest neighbours are a farm field away on one side and a fifteen-minute walk in the other direction. Plus, they watch a horse and buggy go by daily, which adds to the pastoral charm. 'It feels like we're on our own little island here,' John says.

Once the severance came through, John and Juli started work on the place almost immediately, in September 2017. The plan was to remove anything that wasn't structural or architectural and start with a clean slate. The biggest changes were the crumbling lathe and plaster on the second floor and the particleboard walls in the kitchen. 'The spaces transformed in such an unexpected way, so we chose to leave the walls as is,' Juli says.

Step by step they slowly added layers to the home. However, nothing is built-in – everything in the kitchen, bedrooms and bathroom is freestanding. 'This house is all about simplicity,' Juli says. Instead of constructing multiple bedrooms and adding walls within the large vaulted room upstairs, the family all sleep in one room. 'The building spoke of what it wanted us to do,' Juli says. They use a wood-burning stove for heat and cooking. 'Our time spent here is all about being intentional,' she says. The couple haven't been in a hurry, either, in part because it isn't their primary residence. 'The process became intuitive,' John says. 'For some people it's a race to the finish, but it's nice to take it slow.'

The first time they slept in the house was over a long weekend in May 2018. Even though the kitchen was still under construction, they were excited to stay overnight. 'The lilacs and apple blossoms were out and it was heavenly,' Juli says. Work on the house continued that year, with final renovations to the kitchen made in December, just in time for Christmas. 'In the city I find that all the seasons blend together, but here we get to experience all of them individually, each providing us with a unique experience,' Juli says.

In summer they enjoy spending time outside on the patio, and working in the garden. Sitting in front of the large picture window in the living room is another favourite spot. 'It's a nature show,' Juli says. 'And a view that never gets old.'

prestige hi fi lp. 7034
LES DAVIS
JACKSON
QUINTET / SEXTET
axel vervoordt

When I do less…
I feel present. Sometimes I think to myself that I should be doing something, but it somehow feels okay to do absolutely nothing in this place. It's like a dream.

When I disconnect…
life comes into focus. Though this is still a work in progress because we do have our phones, so we find ourselves distracted by them.

I have learnt to live without…
immediate convenience, though this doesn't seem to really affect us that much. One just has to plan ahead and be willing to be flexible.

I set boundaries around…
doing anything I don't want to do.

Calm is…
a challenging place to get to with a puppy and two small children, but when we do experience it, it is golden. The kids are in the creative zone, the puppy is napping and I can just be.

Change is…
continuous. Personally, I invite it through learning and growth; however, in day-to-day life I find change is a challenge.

When it comes to order and chaos in my life…
chaos wins out more frequently than I'd like. It simultaneously feels as if we have too much yet nothing on the go, since we are homebodies.

I care less about…
travel and being out and about. I am thinking more mindfully about the impact we have on the earth and the collective relentless need to pursue more.

I care more about…
living in the moment with my family.

My life feels meaningful when…
my children are engaged and enjoying each other's company, my husband is energised and in the creative flow, my employees are happy and I am evolving.

What's most important in my life right now is…
finding my flow.

**EMBRACING SLOW –
SUSTAINABLE, LOCAL, ORGANIC, WHOLE:**

Sustainable living means…
buying mindfully – choosing items of quality and making decisions that will be long-lasting. With all of our renovation, we focused on timeless options using natural materials for longevity.

Local is…
supporting businesses in your area before big box stores and online.

Organic is…
food and items made with the cycle of consumption in mind.

I feel Whole when…
I'm surrounded by my family and we're all feeling connected.

TANYA JONSSON

Pound Ridge, New York, USA

'Every day I witness the landscape changing
and waking up. I love how the seasons
directly affect the mood of my home;
it's my greatest inspiration.'

Pound Ridge made a lasting impression on
Tanya Jonsson when she visited many years ago.
At the time she was producing her first fashion
photography shoot. 'I loved the area, although
I had no idea where it was,' she says. 'It just felt
you were really far away from everything.' So when
Tanya and her husband, Kris Isacsson, a writer for
film and television, decided to look for a home in
Connecticut about ten years ago, they explored
Pound Ridge, which is just over the border in
New York State.

The couple were ready to leave their Brooklyn
apartment and wanted to find a family home with
a sense of space to raise their daughter, Liv, who was
seven months old at the time. 'We thought it was
time to make a big change,' Tanya says. They found
a 1974 prefab house, typical of many in the region.
'It had a good energy,' she says. 'And we could see
the potential.' The open floor plan of the living area
was appealing, as were the two acres of land and
access to a lake. 'I have surrendered both to the
house and to the landscape, as well as the animals
and insects,' Tanya says. 'You have to embrace it all.
I can fall asleep to an owl hooting all night, and the
bullfrogs at the lake are hysterical. You just have
to succumb to it because you're never going to win.'

Tanya is all too aware that people can easily
become obsessed with perfection when it comes
to their homes and environments. She works as an
interior design director at the esteemed New York
design firm Roman and Williams. For many clients
she is required to create a house from start to finish.
'It can be a wonderful and interesting experience,'
she says. 'However, when I look around my house
I see my life. I see some things that I might not
buy if I saw them again now, but they remind me
of who I was at that time. Even if my taste changes,
there will always be a part of me that's connected
to these objects. And if it isn't, I send it back into
the universe and someone else will love it.'

Tanya has been a collector of art, sculpture and
furniture for more than twenty years. Most of her
finds have come from estate sales, as well as eBay
and Etsy. 'Most of the things I buy have had many
owners,' she says. 'I feel that they've had a life and
are better quality.' Tanya admits much of what she
has bought wouldn't be affordable in the current
marketplace, as vendors are now more aware and
savvy to their provenance and currency. Although,
these are not factors that influence her to buy
something; the connection is more instinctual.
Tanya enjoys the process of working with what she
has. 'It's like a laboratory; I can have failures and
successes – I just edit myself until it feels good,'
she says. 'I love being surrounded by things that
have memories, that move me, that inspire me.'

Tanya became captivated with the process of
creating interiors after she and Kris bought two
small apartments in 2002 and combined them.
An architect friend drew up the plans for them,
recommended a contractor and wished them good
luck. After decorating the home, Tanya completed
an intense year of study at Parsons and learnt the
rest on the job. 'Being in the workforce and loving
it and then devouring the information was the best
education,' she says. 'I always say to younger people
that even if you have a smaller apartment you still
have to play. In my home this is where I can make
mistakes, engage in experiments and have some fun.
And I daydream about what I would love to do to
the house, too.'

Structurally the home remains mostly untouched
from when the couple moved in. However, they
painted both the interior and exterior, and removed
a spiral staircase, loft and sliding glass door from
the living area. Tanya spends a large proportion of
her time working, travelling and creating interiors
for other people, so when she's at home on the
weekends she enjoys spending time with her family,
foraging in the garden and engaging with their
local community.

The area is in the commuter belt, close to a
regular train service with quiet carriages that carry
professionals to New York City. But there are also
many weekenders, as people seek closer alternatives
to the Hamptons and Upstate New York. 'All of
our friends are expat people from Brooklyn who
are looking for the atypical suburban experience,'
Tanya says. 'But there are a lot more artsy and urban
people here than you might expect, who also love
nature and embrace the landscape of Pound Ridge.'

The town remains an important part of the appeal in living here. 'I love that it's a little sleepy, and that our daughter is able to maintain a little bit of innocence here,' Tanya says.

Liv, who is now nine, enjoys foraging with Tanya in amongst the oak trees. 'She says, "Mum, you're crazy," but I hope some of the crazy is rubbing off in a good way,' Tanya says. 'I encourage her to be present and take a look. I feel vindicated when she says, "Mummy, look at that sunset, look at that tree." I feel I've done a good job that she's looking, not always, but she's looking.'

As for the house, thanks to its scale and wall of windows, it brings the outside in and encourages its inhabitants to embrace the landscape and the changing seasons. 'In summer the oak leaf canopy and high sun bring an intense pop of green into our home,' Tanya says. 'Fall creates a gorgeous display of yellows and reds. Winter is icy white and blues. The bare branches and low sun create the most extraordinary shadows. And spring is so exciting. Being immersed in nature is the greatest gift,' Tanya says. 'Nothing brings calm like the sounds of nature around me.'

When I do less…
I feel present. Finding moments each day
to be present is something I strive for.

When I disconnect…
I'm usually in nature, either foraging in the
woods, working in the yard or just taking
a walk. I experience such clarity when I'm
in nature.

I have learnt to live without…
fear of making a mistake. No one likes to
make mistakes, but I have learnt far more
from my mistakes than my successes.

I set boundaries around…
my work schedule. When I come home from
work each night I focus on time with my
family. Emails can wait until the morning.

Calm is…
just being.

Change is…
welcomed. I don't see change as a bad thing.
I think it's really important to understand
how to embrace change in our lives.

When it comes to order and chaos
in my life…
they ebb and flow. For me, too much order
stifles creativity, and I've learnt not to let
chaos overwhelm me.

I care less about…
trends. I look for inspiration in my travels,
art, history and nature. I strive to fill my life
with objects that will inspire my family and
me forever.

I care more about…
quality. A collected life is far more interesting
than an instant one.

My life feels meaningful when…
I see my daughter becoming an intelligent,
strong, kind and willful individual.

What's most important in my life
right now is…
to never stop learning and growing.
Now and always.

**EMBRACING SLOW –
SUSTAINABLE, LOCAL, ORGANIC, WHOLE:**

Sustainable living means…
doing your part to live respectfully with the
planet. Recycle and re-use are big ones for me.

Local is…
supporting your community.

Organic is…
life coming together and growing naturally.
The word is often associated with food, but
living organically can be your life ethos.

I feel Whole when…
I'm being creative in all aspects of my life.

FELIPE HESS & CRIS THOMPSON

São Paulo, Brazil

'Life is good when I am doing nothing, just listening to music, watching my son play and staying in silence beside my wife.'

São Paulo is large and dense – the most populated city in Brazil and also one of the most heavily populated metro areas on the planet. A short distance from its iconic towering skyscrapers is the Jardins district – a name derived from the Portuguese word for 'gardens' – which was farmland up until the 1920s and is now known for the greenery that surrounds the area's low-rise buildings. Architect Felipe Hess moved into one of the district's older homes in 2017 with his wife, Cris, a fashion designer, and their son, Otto, five. 'We have always loved the neighbourhood, and we needed a bigger place,' Felipe says. 'We searched for a while until we found this charming late-1930s house.'

Felipe has a passion for design classics. When it comes to older homes, he is drawn to their good light and proportions. 'Plus, they carry the history of the city and neighbourhood,' he says. The house is not large – it only has two bedrooms and a small kitchen – but its modest size was part of its appeal. 'It's cosy,' Felipe says. 'I can be in the living room while Cris and Otto are in the kitchen and we are still connected. It's essential to us.'

The house spills out onto a garden – something that isn't taken for granted in a city known more for its towering apartment blocks than its green spaces. 'It is a calm and well-located area,' Felipe says. 'We used to live nearby and always came here to walk, ride bikes and go to the local park. Now we are closer to Otto's school and Cris's office and store, Tom Peppers, which are only a walkie-talkie distance from our house. That's considered quality of life in São Paulo.'

Being able to walk to most places has helped the family to slow down and enjoy life more. 'The fact that we don't have to drive around town in the heavy traffic makes everything calmer,' Felipe says. They have also found a strong sense of community in the area. Having a young child has made it easy to forge connections with other families. 'It is a small community and everyone helps each other. And there are always children for Otto to play with,' he says.

After the couple found the home they only made moderate changes, in part because it is a rental but also because they wanted to honour the building. The floor was painted white and the kitchen and bathroom were remodelled, some windows were opened up and storage was added. 'I would never move into something already renovated by someone else,' Felipe says. 'I was looking for personality. Finding something old with an essence, or soul, made sense for us.'

The couple were primarily drawn to the home's connection between inside and outside, so they focused their energies on transforming the garden into a space they could all enjoy. Cris enjoys gardening and often spends time outdoors nurturing her plants, while Felipe uses the space to relax and unwind from the working week. He also designed a contemporary weatherproof pavilion within the garden for Otto to use as an outside playroom. 'When we were living in an apartment we would have to go out a lot with Otto,' Cris says. 'Here, we can just stay and enjoy the space.'

Inside, Cris's favourite room for relaxing is the front living room because of its light and views out to the garden. Felipe prefers to read or listen to music in one of several chairs he has collected over the years. 'I can't find contemporary pieces that are as simple or provide a solution that's as good as the old ones,' he says. 'The quality of the materials, the connections, junctions and fabrics – everything is better from that period.'

The couple enjoy supporting local art and design. As an architect and afficionado of mid-century furniture, Felipe has many Brazilian masterpieces from that period. Their home also has an edited selection of Brazilian contemporary art, collected over the years from when Cris worked as an art dealer. But when asked what was most important when it comes to home life, Felipe answers without hesitation: 'the three of us together'.

When I do less…
I feel I should do it more often. But at the
moment I don't. The only thing I do less at
the moment is sleep.

When I disconnect…
I have a feeling of freedom, especially when
I'm driving my vintage 1970s car, hoping it
gets to the destination.

I have learnt to live without…
an iPod and Spotify. I love my CD collection.

I set boundaries around…
my clients – at least I'm trying to.

Calm is…
part of my nature.

Change is…
also part of my nature.

When it comes to order and chaos
in my life…
I deal well with both. My life is a good
balance of them.

I care less about…
technology.

I care more about…
my family.

My life feels meaningful when…
I get home early from work and can spend
time with Cris and Otto.

What's most important in my life
right now is…
my family.

**EMBRACING SLOW –
SUSTAINABLE, LOCAL, ORGANIC, WHOLE:**

Sustainable living means…
living surrounded with original pieces.
You don't always have to buy new.

Local is…
gold. I always look out for precious local
pieces whenever I travel to a new place.

Organic is…
the future.

I feel Whole when…
I am listening to a new album on my CD player,
and have a good book and a good beer.

BRONWYN & ANDREAS RIEDEL

Saxony, Germany

'The pace of life is of our own making. We're in a quiet place, which is very peaceful and very green. This house is a refuge. I can't imagine living anywhere else.'

Being able to bring life back to an old German manor house was an irresistible opportunity for Bronwyn and Andreas Riedel when they discovered a thirteenth-century *schloss* in the region of Saxony about ten years ago. At the time the couple were living in Western Australia and decided to visit the property during a European holiday. 'It was like falling in love with someone,' Bronwyn says.

They decided to buy it the moment they saw it. Initially it was to become a holiday house and a base when visiting Andreas's family in nearby Dresden, but it was also a working project from the start because of its state of disrepair. There was no water or electricity, no bathrooms or toilet. 'It was awful inside. It was full of rubbish and broken windows,' Bronwyn says. And all seventy-two of them needed to be repaired.

The *schloss* is intricately linked with the history of Germany. The oldest part of the building was once a knight's castle and the former moat is now part of a lake at the rear of the house. 'If you have an understanding of this place within history, it makes more sense and gives it more meaning,' Andreas says. 'The house slowly reveals its past, and it's nice to unearth that.' The existing structure, which comprises twenty rooms, was created in about 1850 and is part of a 380-hectare land parcel. However, the building hadn't been a family home since before World War II. 'And even then it was only a weekender for someone who had a bigger house elsewhere,' Bronwyn says. After that, as part of post-war forced migration, the building was home to seventeen families. Then it became a primary school from the 1950s to 1970s, and Communist propaganda from that era remains painted on a wall in the hallway. Over time, some of the original features were lost, such as the old stairs, which are now lined with terrazzo. After the fall of the Berlin Wall, the *schloss* had quite a few owners. 'But no one did anything with it,' Bronwyn says. 'It just got in a worse and worse state.'

Making the home liveable was a priority. Because winter temperatures can drop to −20°C (−4°F), one of the couple's first projects was to activate the fireplace. 'And we made a promise that if we bought the house, we had to be relaxed about the process,' Bronwyn says. Holidays were spent stripping back the walls, and furnishing it with whatever they could find. They didn't bother with curtains, though, given the outlook onto three hectares of private garden.

'We used to come once a year, and then we started coming more often,' Bronwyn says. During that time they did a lot of invisible work, such as getting all the services up and running. 'If you can't see that we've touched it, I'm happy,' Andreas says. 'I enjoy bringing buildings that were once loved back to life. Our job is not to finish the building but to pass it on.'

About two years ago, Bronwyn and Andreas moved into the house permanently and established a European base for their lime paint business, Bauwerk Colour, which they run from part of the ground floor. 'Even if we don't do another thing, the house is beautiful just as it is,' Bronwyn says. 'And despite having a paint company, we won't paint any of the walls. The more we're here, the less we feel the need to change it.' Besides, every room is a project in itself. 'You tend not to do it as quickly as you would otherwise. As we go along, we let the building tell us what to do next.'

As the couple have learnt more about the *schloss*, they've enjoyed the reconnection formed with the local community. They discovered, for example, that their plumber and electrician both attended the primary school when it was located here. More recently, during winter when the lake was frozen, Bronwyn and Andreas placed flyers in letterboxes throughout the local village, inviting everyone to join them for ice-skating on the pond. 'I like that people still live in a community way,' Bronwyn says. 'They remain private but they keep their civic engagement – if you need help, people will help. I admire them. They live in an uncomplicated way.'

The couple consider themselves custodians of the property. 'We want to think of what we leave behind for the next generation,' Andreas says. 'The house has sustained generations and will sustain many more to come.' Ten years since buying the *schloss*, Bronwyn says she still can't believe she lives here. 'It brings us a lot of joy,' she says. 'There's so much beauty in the old windows and walls with how they've been built. I often think of who lived here before and what they did. Your imagination can be really free in a place like this.'

When I do less…
I feel relaxed. Having time to dream is my favourite thing – I feel energised and excited.

When I disconnect…
I have a sense of freedom to be able to wander in my own world for a little while.

I have learnt to live without…
chasing life – trying to make things happen. I'm still ambitious and connected to what I'm doing, but I'm able to let go of my insecurities.

I set boundaries around…
what I do well, and try to be aware of what I can contribute and what is best left to others.

Calm is…
having a space to dream. Coming here is like coming back to my childhood in the country – I spent a lot of time dreaming and imagining things. I enjoy the space here to do that again.

Change is…
something I like. Life changes quite a lot at different stages and I have learnt that it's good and it's fine. Even if things don't go the way you think, something better comes along. I'm happy to go my own way and back myself. I've learnt that whatever happens, I'll be okay. In fact, I find life tends to turn out better.

When it comes to order and chaos in my life…
it's a fine line. I tend to err more towards order, but I can be quite chaotic. We are all a balance of both. I couldn't live in a house like this and stress about having it perfect, because it wouldn't work. And while I do try to do things really well, I've learnt it's better to get them done rather than try to do them perfectly.

I care less about…
being someone I'm not. In my youth I was crippled by wanting to do things so well that it held me back. I had to learn not to be so hard on myself. I care less about doing something 'wrong'. I say, 'Do your best and be thoughtful and kind – you can't do much more than that.'

I care more about…
feeling that I can contribute to my family, friends and community. I really believe in the product we make and what we do.

My life feels meaningful when…
I'm connected to people and what I do on a daily basis. When things flow, I get excited about new projects and interactions with people. Working successfully as a family has been the most wonderful gift to my life.

What's most important in my life right now is…
developing the ideas that I have: growing our business, developing this property into the things we dream of. I love to introduce people to this part of Germany because I feel it's undiscovered and unappreciated.

EMBRACING SLOW –
SUSTAINABLE, LOCAL, ORGANIC, WHOLE:

Sustainable living means…
everything has to be sustainable: how you look after yourself, the people you work with, and the decisions you make in your business. We should all be thinking about the next generation.

Local is…
everything. If I can't buy local, I buy from people who care about what they do. Local is also where you live. It's really important – the community in which you live is the backbone of your life.

Organic is…
something I've always been attracted to. I grew up on a farm that grew organic vegetables. I appreciate organic materials and experiences – and interactions. You can't plan for everything. Some things just happen. Our business grew organically. Organic is the best in all scenarios.

I feel Whole when…
I'm with my family and friends. And when I'm in a creative headspace, when everything is flowing well, which makes me feel energised.

REINHOLD HERRMANN
und welt und traum
COLLAGEN

TIME-HONOURED METHODS

The materials we choose when creating a home play an important role in our experience of a place. They can also have a profound impact on the environment, now and into the future. Bronwyn and Andreas Riedel of Bauwerk Colour want to change our relationship with one of the most common materials used in homes – paint. Almost twenty years ago, they became makers and advocates for a product that works in harmony with nature and can enhance our experience of how we live at home.

Bronwyn Riedel

We are driven by a belief that we should have a greater connection to the materials we use in our homes. We are passionate about the layers we add and how we connect to them emotionally and physically. This philosophy is behind everything we do.

How a home feels is sometimes intangible; we can experience homes almost instinctively. They were once created from the natural materials sourced around them, and those materials, like most things in nature, were perfect because they came from the environment in which people lived. Often they suited the climate and the needs of the people living within them; they were designed to take nature into consideration. There are, of course, many wonderful modern improvements, but we believe that not everything we have introduced into our buildings is necessary or indeed desirable.

All walls that are made from brick, masonry, stone and other natural materials – if they are constructed correctly – have the capacity to naturally store and release moisture and humidity. This improves indoor air quality and the longevity of the built structure, keeping all elements of the building in harmony with one another. When we were working in building restoration, we noticed that many chemical materials used on walls, such as oil paints and water-based acrylics, were hard to remove and had often damaged the underlying structure of the building.

One of nature's most beautiful natural materials is limestone, or calcium carbonate (its chemical name), which starts its life as sea shells. Our lifelong love affair with this material, and its many wonderful qualities, began more than thirty years ago. We saw that when limewashes were used in historical buildings the walls stayed permeable – meaning the walls could still breathe. Unfortunately, modern wall coatings create a plastic or oil-coating barrier, and this results in problems of damp. We believe this barrier is like putting a plastic bag over your skin, and just as that creates an infection or a bigger problem, it is the same on buildings; when moisture is trapped within the substrate, then the same festering of the surface occurs. This may be disguised for some time, as the coating will mask it, but eventually a much larger problem will surface.

The use of modern coatings in this way also impacts greatly on our indoor air quality and groundwater. Many conventional house paints can take several years to stop off-gassing. The chemicals that are used to make them work as coatings – made using plastic, oil and biocides including formaldehyde – release gas into the air. Conventional paints also require a large amount of water to clean up, with the residue going straight into our groundwater.

Not everyone can or wants to live in an old limestone house. However, wherever we live, good materials and an understanding of how they interact with one another can make a big difference to the choices we make when constructing and renovating a home. Natural materials provide a beautiful way to live that goes beyond fashion and trends – one of the most notable differences is the air quality and the 'feel' of the room. We have walked into many new projects constructed using bricks, masonry or stone, which are then rendered and painted with limewash, and we are always surprised at how pleasant the air and room feel. It is hard to describe in words, but it's really noticeable.

Traditionally, limewashed walls were repainted yearly, not because the paint isn't long-lasting but because the paint also has a natural alkalinity and antibacterial qualities that help protect the walls and building.

So began our discovery of the beauty of limewash, and a desire to create a paint that is naturally beautiful and in harmony with nature. One of our most important decisions has been that what we leave out is more important than what we put in. Our limewash is made by a perfect alchemy of earth, fire, water and air. Limestone comes from the earth, and is then heated in a unique burning process that changes the chemical composition. It is slaked in water and then aged for many years – just like good wine, the limewash gets better with time. It is now ready to be made into limewash paint. Once painted onto walls, it takes carbon dioxide from the air and, in a completely natural process, turns back into limestone, or calcium carbonate, and dries on the wall.

The next step is the colouring, which we also do using a 'less is more' philosophy. We are equally fascinated by pigments and their natural beauty; the way they all have their own characteristics based upon where they come from and their mineral composition. We use an artist's approach to colouring, not an industrial one – what is it, where does it come from, what are its tones. We don't offer paints that come from harmful chemicals such as cadmium, which is used to create bright yellow, red and orange. We also don't use any bright pink because the pigment is very detrimental to those using it in paint manufacturing.

Paint colours are usually created by an industrial process with pigments bound into acrylic/plastic or oil-based mediums. We bypass the use of these binders. One of the most delightful results of colouring this way is the light refraction that happens between pigments and limestone: when you look at limestone under a microscope you can see millions of crystals, which bounce light back in a unique way. This, combined with the pigments, creates luminosity and colour that looks and is experienced differently. It creates whites that are brilliant but not harsh, as it bounces the light back in a much softer way.

The wonder of limewash never ceases to delight and amaze us.

BRONWYN RIEDEL has worked as a textile designer and taught colour theory and textile design. Andreas worked as a stonemason on historical buildings in Dresden, Germany, before migrating to Australia, where he met Bronwyn. Together they worked on many restoration projects before starting Bauwerk Colour in 2000 in Fremantle, Western Australia. Today they live and work in Saxony, Germany.

JAN ELENI LEMONEDES
& RONNIE STAM

Trancoso, Brazil

'I believe in starting your day with gratitude,
gentle deep breathing and visualisations.
Incorporating this into my daily life provides
a chance to self-reflect. This awareness –
the inner observation, the sincerity within
yourself – is the very basis for slow living.'

About ten years ago, Jan Eleni Lemonedes,
Ronnie Stam and their daughter, Lola, first visited
Trancoso, a tropical hideaway along the Bahia coast
of Brazil. 'When we arrived, we were quickly swept
up by village life and the kindness shown to us.
The place felt authentic and had a bohemian quality
that we both loved,' Jan says. 'We felt so far removed
from our life in New York, but also had a sense that
we were on a wonderful journey and adventure.'

Within days they started looking at available
houses to buy close to the Quadrado, a grassy
square lined with fishermen's huts overlooking
the sea and mangroves. At the end of the square
stands Brazil's second oldest church, built by Jesuit
priests who founded the village in the late 1500s.
'During our ten-day stay our hearts became full,
and we signed the necessary papers to help start the
buying process, just in case one of the houses came
through,' Jan says.

At the time the couple were living fast-paced lives
in New York. Jan was working as a creative project
manager for ABC Carpet and Home, and Ronnie,
originally from The Netherlands, was immersed in
the fashion industry freelancing as a hair stylist on
shoots around the world for top-tier magazines.
A year after their visit to Trancoso, 9/11 struck and
Jan decided to take time out to spend more time
with their young daughter. After Lola turned five,
Jan started creating children's spaces for clients in
Manhattan, which then led to interior design work.

One of the attractions of making a home within
the beachside community was to give their family
a foundation and a focal point. 'Lola was ten at
the time, and I wanted to give her memories and
a connection to a place – there's an openness in
Bahia and an inclusiveness here,' Jan says. 'Plus it
was a wonderful opportunity to experience another
culture.' When a property a short walk from the
main square came up, they took it. The couple
signed the papers in November 2010 and visited

Trancoso four times that year, working closely
with a local architect to build Casa Lola. To make
the purchase possible they decided, like others
in the area, to make it available for short-term
holiday lettings.

'We had a strong sense of what we wanted –
nothing too overpowering for the space or the
street,' Jan says. For the original cottage, they
followed the traditional rustic-style fishermen's
houses, similar to the ones in the Quadrado. They
recycled and re-used old roof tiles to add to the
authentic feeling. For the new house, built on
the opposite side of the pool, they wanted an airy
space, reflecting something of their NYC loft-style
living, but incorporating down-to-earth Trancoso
rustic elements. A few years ago they bought the
neighbour's cottage and converted that into a
garden hideaway house, one that would blend with
nature. They planted more garden, jaboticaba and
banana trees, and added a pergola where they can
cook and entertain outdoors.

Trancoso has a bohemian feel, thanks in part
to hippies who moved into the area in the 1970s.
'It seemed only natural that Casa Lola would have
that beach-easy, raw-earthy, rustic-boho vibe,' Jan
says. The couple also cite renowned Japanese–
American sculptor and designer Isamu Noguchi as
an influence. 'We have always admired and found
great inspiration from his muted mix of raw, rustic
and natural elements,' Jan says. They combined
these ideas with elements found within local homes,
and employed the *madeira envelhecida* technique to
provide a weathered appearance to timber.

Most of the house's creation has involved local
artisans and materials. The craftsmen of Trancoso
made the furniture using Brazilian woods, including
locally grown eucalyptus, which was used for all
four beds and the sofa in the living room, as well
as the drainage gutters throughout the property.
In Trancoso, fallen trees are often utilised and
repurposed, which inspired Jan and Ronnie to
put this idea into play when creating an outside
shower. They also used tree and branch offcuts as
the casing for a showerhead and bath spout inside
the cottage. Copper taps and wooden shutters
were also made locally.

'The community here has become our extended
family,' Jan says. When they visit, they love to catch
up with friends and neighbours. Ronnie has done

many charity haircut sessions in the Quadrado, giving the proceeds to a few local causes. Jan and Lola have also contributed to the community by teaching young children English. 'We care deeply for the people around us,' Jan says. 'They are an important part of our Trancoso life.'

Equally, life at Casa Lola is an opportunity to slow down. 'When we are here we unplug, and plug into nature,' Jan says. 'Once you are here you can't help but slow down. There is something in the air – the sounds, the smells, the food, the people – your senses become heightened, and the idea of time ebbs away.'

Jan Eleni Lemonedes & Ronnie Stam

When I do less…
I feel rejuvenated, renewed and alive.

When I disconnect…
it creates freedom for me to connect to what's
most important in my life – family and friends,
and being in tune to myself and the rhythms
of nature and life.

I have learnt to live without…
foods containing more than five ingredients.
I follow the wholefood way.

I set boundaries around…
people with negative energy.

Calm is…
finding your inner peace.

Change is…
exciting, as it creates versatility.

When it comes to order and chaos
in my life…
each needs the other to complete the
balance cycle.

I care less about…
having more.

I care more about…
family, friends, the ocean and, of course,
laughing.

My life feels meaningful when…
we can all – Ronnie, Lola and myself –
be together for an extended length of time.

What's most important in my life
right now is…
watching my daughter blossom into an
independent, strong, sensitive, liberal woman,
while maintaining her strong values and
fearless quality.

**EMBRACING SLOW –
SUSTAINABLE, LOCAL, ORGANIC, WHOLE:**

Sustainable living means…
to have a deep moral sense and love for
Mother Earth, and passing that knowledge
on to the next generation.

Local is…
supporting, sharing and communicating with
your neighbours and the community within
which you live.

Organic is…
an approach to our everyday lives. How we
eat, live, work, sleep – trying to do this at its
purest level.

I feel Whole when…
I am in sync with myself; this equals healthy
body and healthy mind.

Jan Eleni Lemonedes

ANDREA DEL GENIO

Grottaglie, Puglia, Italy

'A *masseria* is the heart of a farm and part of a culture that goes back thousands of years. A *masseria* without a farm is just stone for me. However, we need to create them in a modern way while still respecting the past. The idea is to have the centre of my life in the centre of the farm, like it was 100 years ago.'

There is a strong sense of history and a respect for the future in the home of Andrea del Genio. He lives in the southern Italian region of Puglia in the village of Grottaglie on land that has been part of his family for 300 years. And while the property is firmly rooted in the past, he has created a *masseria* – a farmhouse – that can be passed on to future generations. Since moving here, Andrea has transformed abandoned stone buildings into liveable spaces that he shares with workers and travellers from around the world. However, the evolution of the site has been slow and considered.

Andrea was born and raised in Naples, and worked at one of its universities as an assistant professor of Economic History. It was around 2000, when his grandmother turned ninety, that the family began to talk about selling the *masseria*. 'I decided I would visit my grandma to help out on the farm for fifteen days. And twenty years later, I'm still here,' he says. 'My friends were working in the USA, London and Geneva, and they all said I was crazy for staying. And now it's the opposite.'

No one had been living in the *masseria* since World War II. 'It was too far in the countryside for my family to live,' Andrea says. 'The land was just a place to come and work and then go back. But I decided to be here because it's more in keeping with the idea of agriculture to live here with the plants. I understand more about them each day.'

At first he stayed in a nearby village as the stone buildings on the farm weren't habitable. The priority was to focus on making the farm a viable business so he would then have the funds to restore the buildings at a later date. 'Originally my grandmother's father used the land for growing almonds. Then my grandmother grew grapes for the table and I decided to grow grapes for wine,' he says. Olives and cereals, such as wheat and barley, are also harvested.

When Andrea first arrived at the farm he spent a lot of time observing the workers. 'No one understood why I was just watching,' he says. 'Then – it's like music – when you start to study piano, step by step the music comes inside you. It is the same with agriculture. But it's also a science, and work.' Shortly after he started working on the farm, he decided to change from conventional to organic agriculture. 'I was one of the first in this area,' he says. 'A lot of people said it wasn't a good idea, but life is not just about money. While it is important to live, you need to have some ethics – and you *can* have a business with values.'

About five years ago, Andrea had enough funds to update the buildings, including some that housed sheep and cows. The main building, where he lives and works, had also been derelict, but the foundations and structure were in good condition. The floors were formed from large blocks of stone that are each about 40 centimetres deep and 40 kilograms in weight. 'They were made for more than one generation,' he says. 'In the past they were building for the future. It was a different way of thinking. In a way, it's more ecological.' As part of the rebuilding process, Andrea's team removed all the floors and created space underneath so air could circulate. 'The Romans were doing this thousands of years ago,' he says.

The style of the building is typical of the area. The use of stone makes sense in many ways: as a local material it's easy to access, and its thermal properties help to keep homes cool. Also, the use of high ceilings allows hot air to rise. 'The original stonework would have taken thousands of hours of work. Each piece would have been cut by hand, not by machine,' Andrea says. 'It's unbelievable how in the past they built something that we can still live in and be comfortable in today.'

Three years ago Andrea opened some of the buildings within the *masseria* into an agritourism business, Masseria Celano. 'Celano' comes from the ancient Greek word for 'turtle': this part of Italy was colonised by the Ancient Greeks and was known as Magna Graecia, and before the use of machines there were many turtles on the land. 'Opening Masseria Celano to guests was good for me because the things I love most in life are agriculture and travelling. Unfortunately, with organic farming I can't travel much, as I have to be with my plants,' Andrea says. 'So, in a way, I can travel through the guests in my house, as I get to meet people from all over the world.'

Andrea del Genio

When I do less…
I feel I must have balance. There is a saying that in the moment of rest you work better than when you work. Most religions have one day without work and it's important to understand that humans are not machines – we need to rest.

When I disconnect…
I am more connected with people.

I have learnt to live without…
the theatre of life, without chaos.

I set boundaries around…
love. You must have moments when you are within a couple that you can be alone together, and not have the rest of the world with you.

Calm is…
something you have inside the heart. You can have it when living among the chaos of a city or on the land. You can be calm whether you're living in Masseria Celano, Bombay or Beijing – when you have it within, it doesn't matter where you live.

Change is…
the best thing in life because we can see the world from a completely different side. Everybody can experience a different point of view. It's pure energy.

When it comes to order and chaos in my life…
I have both. When you understand that you cannot control everything in life, you are in order, because it is in this position that you understand life.

I care less about…
what other people think about me.

I care more about…
my way to be in the world. In Italian, we talk about *sinestesia* – synaesthesia. We have the *dolce* 'sweet' and *amaro* 'bitter' together.

My life feels meaningful when…
I try to leave the world a little bit better than when I got here.

What's most important in my life right now is…
love.

**EMBRACING SLOW –
SUSTAINABLE, LOCAL, ORGANIC, WHOLE:**

Sustainable living means…
to not destroy the fertility of the land and with it the possibility of a new generation living in our world. My motto is from the Latin, *festina lente* (or *affrettati lentamente* in Italian) – make haste slowly.

Local is…
something that is from a place but from the world at the same time. A population is never from a place. In Italy we have a population from all over the world. On my farm there are people from all over the world. Local is a fusion that comes from other parts of the world. The concept of local is in the world and the world is in local.

Organic is…
a way of producing with more respect for nature. It affects not just the way you farm but how you consider your role as a human on the planet, because as a good organic farmer you must also change the way you see the world. It's a process that goes together.

I feel Whole when…
I do a good day of work, and drink a good wine with some friends.

ABOUT THE AUTHOR

Natalie Walton is a designer and creative director focused on a simple idea – reclaiming the true beauty of our lives. As founder of Imprint House, a design studio based in Byron Bay, Australia, she brings this philosophy to life. Together with her team, she creates genuine and atmospheric interiors, meaningful products that embrace the principles of SLOW living, and emotional connections to story for brands and business through her range of courses, including The Styling Masterclass. These ideas are distilled in her first book *This is Home: The Art of Simple Living.*

nataliewalton.com

ABOUT THE PHOTOGRAPHER

Chris Warnes is one of Australia's leading interior photographers known for capturing well-crafted and soulful images. His work has been featured in a range of leading publications across the globe, including *Vogue Living, Elle Decoration UK* and *Living Etc.* Chris works with architects, interior designers as well as advertising clients on a range of diverse projects. His fine art photography is available through the gallery Otomys. This is the second book he has photographed, following on from *This is Home: The Art of Simple Living.*

chriswarnes.com.au

An open door, a warm welcome and an in-depth conversation with the following people around the world helped to make this book possible.

Alejandro Sticotti and
Mercedes Hernáez
Buenos Aires,
Argentina
sticotti.net
tiendamono.com
p 53

Ameé and Glen Allsop
East Hampton,
New York, USA
ameeallsop.com
glenallsop.com
p 111

Andrea del Genio
Grottaglie,
Puglia, Italy
masseriacelano.com
p 237

Andrea Moore
Meeniyan, Victoria,
Australia
studiomoore.com.au
p 67

Bronwyn and
Andreas Riedel
Saxony, Germany
bauwerkcolour.com
p 217

Charlotte Minch
Tisvildeleje, Denmark
p 121

Courtney Adamo
Bangalow, NSW,
Australia
courtneyadamo.com
p 103

Elise Pioch Chappell
and Paul Chappell
Béziers, France
maisonbalzac.com
p 145

Emma and Tom Lane
Byron Bay, NSW,
Australia
therangebyronbay.
com.au
p 175

Felipe Hess and
Cris Thompson
São Paulo, Brazil
felipehess.com.br
tompeppers.com.br
p 209

Jan Eleni Lemonedes
and Ronnie Stam
Trancoso, Brazil
casalolatrancoso.com
p 227

Jessica Kraus
San Clemente,
California, USA
houseinhabit.com
p 87

João Rodrigues
Lisbon, Portugal
silentliving.pt
p 33

Juli Daoust Baker
and John Baker
Stirling, Ontario,
Canada
mjolk.ca
p 189

Kasia Bilinski and
Matthew Murphy
Callicoon,
New York, USA
p 77

Kine Ask Stenersen
and Kristoffer Eng
Drammen, Norway
askogeng.no
p 43

Mercedes Lopez
Coello
Moscari, Mallorca,
Spain
p 157

Nina and Craig
Plummer
Edinburgh, Scotland
ingredientsldn.com
p 21

Romi Weinberg
Sydney, Australia
p 133

Tanya Jonsson
Pound Ridge,
New York, USA
p 201

Books are always a good idea. Here are some that informed this one.

In Praise of Slow: How a Worldwide Movement is Challenging the Cult of Speed by Carl Honoré (Orion Books)

Slow: Live Life Simply by Brooke McAlary (Allen & Unwin)

12 Rules for Life: An Antidote to Chaos by Jordan B Peterson (Allen Lane)

The Blue Zones: 9 Lessons for Living Longer from the People Who've Lived the Longest by Dan Buettner (National Geographic)

Start with Why: How Great Leaders Inspire Everyone to Take Action by Simon Sinek (Penguin)

Mindfulness for Beginners: Reclaiming the Present Moment – and Your Life by Jon Kabat-Zinn (Sounds True)

Wherever You Go There You Are: Mindfulness Meditation in Everyday Life by Jon Kabat-Zinn (Hachette Books)

The Power of Now: A Guide to Spiritual Enlightenment by Eckhart Tolle (Yellow Kite)

A New Earth: Create a Better Life by Eckhart Tolle (Penguin)

Strength in Stillness: The Power of Transcendental Meditation by Bob Roth (Simon & Schuster)

Silence – In the Age of Noise by Erling Kagge (Penguin)

AUTHOR'S NOTE

The seed of this book began when my family stayed on an organic farm in the hills behind Verona, Italy, in 2015. At the time we were living in an inner-city terrace in Sydney, Australia. But on that holiday as my husband and I watched our children run through fields of wildflowers we began to reassess what was most important in our lives. We made the decision to move out of the city to the countryside. Living on land gave us a whole new appreciation for our connection with nature. Within two weeks of our move we were flooded in. Thankfully, that lasted only a couple of days, but for the next few years we experienced the other extreme: rainwater tanks – our primary water supply – running dry many times. We also watched bushfires burn within sight of our property. We experienced first hand the cycle of life when we got a rescue dog to ward off snakes and goannas that were eating the eggs of chickens introduced in an attempt to live more sustainably. In the end, the dog killed some of our chickens and the neighbour's too. The goannas and snakes remained. And with sadness we had to surrender the dog. It was a valuable lesson in the fragility of ecosystems. We also spent time walking along the side of the road, sometimes with a wheelbarrow, picking up rubbish that had been thrown out of car windows. This type of blatant disregard for our planet and its inhabitants was shocking. But it was something I witnessed first hand in several countries throughout the trip to create this book. In the USA, Canada and Italy I watched people toss rubbish out of car windows. I travelled on planes on which single-use plastic was handed out to every passenger with every meal and drink. I walked through airports where drink bottles were confiscated at security check points to see vending machines at the other end of the conveyor belts filled with single-use plastic bottles. Every passenger on every flight had to place toiletries into single-use plastic bags. It started to feel as if the world had lost sight of the bigger picture. Even in Italy, where the slow movement began, I felt deep frustration when I bought an espresso at a bar because I didn't want to get a single-use takeaway coffee cup – but the barista handed me an accompanying drink of water in a plastic cup. Years ago I was only ever given a drink of water in a glass. Was the world regressing? Or had I been living in a bubble?

On my return I rewrote large sections of the book because I wanted to do all that I could, and anything that was possible, to help awaken us to what was happening in the world at large. Because many of us do live in a bubble. The world has become increasingly binary, and polarised. But it is our responsibility to become more aware of how we are *all* living and make meaningful change. Sometimes that begins with the smallest steps – saying no to someone who offers us a drink in a plastic cup, taking our own food, using re-usable utensils when possible, picking up rubbish in our neighbourhood, and more. And we can talk about the steps we take. This is my story. I hope that you share yours, too. #myslowhome

CARBON OFFSETS WERE USED FOR ALL FLIGHTS THAT WERE TAKEN TO CREATE THIS BOOK.

THANK YOU

What began as a simple idea for a book has turned into a life manifesto for my family, and hopefully many others. Thank you to Jane Willson, Marg Bowman and the team at Hardie Grant for believing in it from the start, and for your patience with the creation process. Special mention to Evi O Studio for your expert eye and Kim Rowney for your judicious editing.

As with *This is Home*, this book has been made possible thanks to photographer Chris Warnes – not only for his beautiful photos but his insights, support and agreement to travel across continents to chase light and create magic. Forever grateful.

And to the homeowners who helped bring this book to life. Thank you!

Once again, the biggest thanks goes to my husband, Daniel, for going above and beyond many times over to provide the time and space to create this book. And to my children, Charlie, Sabina, Isis and Miles – this book is for you and your future.

A special dedication to John for being a part of the process, and inspiring many of the ideas within this book's pages. Your legacy lives on. Thank you.

Published in 2020 by Hardie Grant Books,
an imprint of Hardie Grant Publishing

Hardie Grant Books (Melbourne)
Building 1, 658 Church Street
Richmond, Victoria 3121

Hardie Grant Books (London)
5th & 6th Floors
52–54 Southwark Street
London SE1 1UN

hardiegrantbooks.com

 A catalogue record for this
book is available from the
National Library of Australia

NATIONAL
LIBRARY
OF AUSTRALIA

Still: The slow home
ISBN 978 1 74379 570 5

10 9 8 7 6 5 4 3 2

Publishing Director: Jane Willson
Managing Editor: Marg Bowman
Editor: Kim Rowney
Design Manager: Jessica Lowe
Designer: Evi O.
Photographer: Chris Warnes
Production Manager: Todd Rechner
Production Coordinator: Mietta Yans

Colour reproduction by Splitting Image Colour Studio
Printed in China by Leo Paper Products LTD.